how2become

A GCHQ Intelligence Analyst

www.how2become.com

Orders: Please contact How2become Ltd, Suite 14, 50 Churchill Square Business Centre, Kings Hill, Kent ME19 4YU.

You can order through Amazon.co.uk under ISBN 9781910602799, via the website www.How2Become. com or through Gardners.com.

ISBN: 9781910602799

First published in 2016 by How2become Ltd.

Typeset by How2become Limited.

Disclaimer

Every effort has been made to ensure that the information contained within this guide is accurate at the time of publication. How2become Ltd are not responsible for anyone failing any part of any selection process as a result of the information contained within this guide. How2become Ltd and their authors cannot accept any responsibility for any errors or omissions within this guide, however caused. No responsibility for loss or damage occasioned by any person acting, or refraining from action, as a result of the material in this publication can be accepted by How2become Ltd.

The information within this guide does not represent the views of any third party service or organisation.

Contents

Introduction
to GCHQ

Hello, and welcome to *How To Become a GCHQ Intelligence Analyst: The Ultimate Guide.* This book has been written to give YOU a head start in your career as an intelligence analyst. Before we begin though, it's important to get you thinking like an analyst. To help you do this, we've constructed a short brain teaser below. Have a go at the puzzle, and see if you can get the correct answer.

Please note

Any puzzles contained within this guide are only there to help you THINK like an analyst. They are not representative of the job that GCHQ analysts do on a regular basis, nor are they designed to mimic any real GCHQ assessment.

GCHQ Brain Teaser, Exercise 1

Every morning, Nathan Parker commutes to his office in London. He arrives at work at 08:45, grabs a coffee and then sits down at his computer. Nathan works in the customer service department of his computing firm. Recently, however, Nathan has grown bored of working there.

Whenever his boss isn't looking, Nathan signs in to his local messaging app to talk to his friend, who uses the same service. In order to disguise their messages, Nathan and his friend talk in a special code. On Monday morning, here is what Nathan said to his friend:

(8,1) : (2,1) : (5,2) : (3,2) : (2,1) : (9,1) : (2,1) : (9,3) – (4,3) : (7,1) : (4,3) : (9,4) : (9,4) : (2,1) – (5,3) : (2,1) : (8,1) : (3,2) : (7,3).

GCHQ Brain Teaser, Exercise 1 Answer

The code for the above sequence is *'Takeaway Pizza Later'*.

Take a look at your phone keypad. Every digit corresponds with a letter.

For example, the 1st letter on the number 8 is a *T* (8,1) and the 1st letter on the number 2 is an *A* (2,1). If you managed to solve this, congratulations!

If you did not manage to solve the brain teaser, don't worry, you'll have plenty more chances to test yourself.

'<u>Digital Firefighters</u>'

The world around us is more dangerous than ever before. England's threat level is set at an unprecedented high, and this shows no sign of abating. Conflicts in the Middle East, along with the rapid improvement of technology in the past decade, mean that Britain is at risk from terrorists and home grown criminals alike. So, how can we stop these people, and protect our citizens? The answer is via national security organisations, such as GCHQ.

GCHQ (Government Communications Headquarters) is a British intelligence agency that operates primarily online, and in conjunction with organisations such as MI5. Their main body of work consists of tracking down and monitoring criminals, such as paedophiles or suspected terrorists. Given the rise of new technology, GCHQ are also fundamental in preventing hacking attacks that could jeopardise the security of Britain. In computing terms, GCHQ are Britain's foremost firewall against digital attacks, and also contribute hugely to the anti-terror movement.

So, what do you need to work for GCHQ? Below we've listed the key eligibility criteria for the role.

<u>GCHQ Eligibility Criteria</u>

Given the importance of GCHQ to national security, it might surprise you to learn that you will not need to meet huge amounts of eligibility criteria in order to work there.

<u>The list you will need to meet is as follows:</u>

- You must be a British citizen, or in the process of applying to become one.

- You must be aged 18 years old or over.

- You must have lived in the UK for the last 10 years, with the exception of serving overseas with the armed forces, representing the government in overseas matters, studying abroad or living abroad with parents.

- At least one of your parents must be a British citizen, or have demonstrable/strong links to the UK.

<u>GCHQ may reject you, if:</u>

- You are being treated for an addiction, such as alcoholism, or have been receiving treatment for this in the last year.

- You have used Class A drugs, such as ecstasy, in the last year.

- You have used Class B or C drugs, such as cannabis, in the last year.

- You are currently bankrupt, or subject to an Individual Voluntary Agreement.

- You have ever suffered from psychotic illness or episodes, or bi-polar.

When applying to GCHQ, you will be subject to *extremely* thorough background checks, in order to ascertain that you are a suitable person for the role. If this list seems fairly limited, don't be fooled. Remember that the people who are applying for the same role as you will generally be extremely qualified and have a very high standard of education/ work experience. While a degree or higher isn't an official requirement, extra qualifications such as these will add hugely to your application. The assessors will look far more favourably upon candidates who can show both educational and work-based skills, meaning that you could really struggle to compete against those who are more qualified than you. In order to give yourself the best chances of success, you will need to go as far as you can to become as qualified as you can, before applying to GCHQ.

Finally, it goes without saying that you will need to be someone who can work discreetly, and maintain a high level of secrecy. Similarly to MI5, GCHQ is an extremely private organisation that relies on maximum secrecy in order to achieve its goals. Given their importance to national security, employees of GCHQ cannot disclose their role to anyone outside of close friends and family. A breach of this would put not only themselves and their family in danger, but the general British public.

One of the most important jobs in GCHQ is to identify and analyse different international threats to the UK. This role is known as **Intelligence Analyst**. As you might have guessed, this is what we'll be focusing on in this book.

In the next chapter, we'll look at exactly what an intelligence analyst does, and give you a brief overview of the selection process.

CHAPTER 1
GCHQ Intelligence Analyst

Now that you've had an introduction to GCHQ, let's take a look at one of the most integral roles in the organisation. Intelligence analysts are responsible for identifying international threats to the UK.

In order to do this, they use a range of analytical tools and devices, including the most up-to-date technology. Once a potential threat has been identified, GCHQ intelligence analysts work in conjunction with other employees in GCHQ, MI5 and sometimes MI6, to determine, deal with and detain the perpetrator.

If you need an example of how effective this is, just think about the following. Given the increase in terrorism in the last 20 years, how many attacks have actually been committed on British soil? Since 2005, Britain has been largely untouched by terrorism (despite many attempts) and this is down to the fantastic work of national intelligence and security services.

In order to track down terrorists, GCHQ intelligence analysts might use any number of methods at their disposal. This could include:

- Tracing IP addresses.

- Tracking mobile numbers.

- Working with other intelligence agencies, such as MI5 or MI6.

- Intercepting and analysing communications between suspected or known threats.

- Using past and current data to ascertain links between different suspects.

- Using behavioural analysis and expert judgement to form logical conclusions on suspects.

Sound difficult? Well, it is. Getting a job in GCHQ is extremely challenging, and only the most elite candidates will successfully pass the selection process.

Here is a short breakdown of the different stages that you will face:

GCHQ Intelligence Analyst: Selection Process

Stage 1: Application Form

Stage 2: Online Tests

Stage 3: Telephone Interview

Stage 4: Assessment Centre

Stage 5: Interview

Stage 6: Further Vetting

Stage 7: Final Interview

As you might have expected, the selection process for GCHQ is extremely tough. While the process can differ between years, and GCHQ are entirely flexible in their approach, the difficulty in gaining a position will be just as hard, if not harder in order to meet the demanding nature of the job.

In particular, you can expect the vetting process to be extremely rigorous, and this can sometimes take a long time to complete. You'll have to supply GCHQ with a range of different documents in order to prove your validity as a candidate, and they will also make contact with past employers to ensure you are a suitable person for the job role to which you have applied.

GCHQ Apprentice and Graduate Scheme

In the past 2 years, GCHQ have stepped up their recruitment campaign for younger people. In order for them to do this, they have introduced a number of different schemes, designed to attract technologically-interested students, apprentices and graduates:

If you are an upcoming graduate or taking a degree in Engineering, Information Technology, Cyber Security, Telecommunications, Physics, Electronics, Computer Science or Information Security, then GCHQ are willing to offer you 11 weeks of paid work in the space between your penultimate and final years of study. This 11 weeks can also be extended to 22 weeks, to continue through the final summer of your course.

Alternatively, GCHQ also offer two different summer schools for graduates and apprentices:

Cyber Exposure 2016

Cyber Exposure 2016 is a 6 week summer school which gives attendees the chance to learn more about the internet, and the way in which GCHQ protect the UK from internal and external threats. Attendees of the course will receive £250 per week, plus free accommodation.

In order to qualify for this summer school, you will need to have a minimum of 2 A-Levels, at grades A-C. You will also need to have a keen interest in problem solving, technology and new gadgets.

Cyber Insider School 2016

Cyber Insider School is an 11 week summer programme, located in Cheltenham. It provides attendees with the chance to gain a fascinating insight into all things cyber. Attendees will learn from world-leading cyber industry experts, on topics such as ethical hacking, operating system defences and more. Attendees of the course will receive £250 per week, plus free accommodation.

In order to qualify for this summer school, you will need to be graduating between summer 2016 and 2019, and must be taking a degree in physics, maths, computer science or another closely related subject.

Before we move onto the initial application form/questionnaire, there are several more important elements to consider, on what makes for a good GCHQ intelligence analyst.

Collectively, these elements are known as the **core competencies**, and will be essential in order for you to pass the selection process, and hold down a job at GCHQ.

Core Competencies

Just as with any employer, GCHQ have a range of core competencies that they will expect their employees to abide by if they wish to a) pass the process, and b) hold down a position as an intelligence analyst.

So, what do we mean by core competencies? Core competencies refer to the key behavioural expectations that an employer has for their employee. In order to gain a job, and succeed within that role, these competencies will be integral. You will need to demonstrate them at every chance you get during the selection process, in order to impress the assessors as much as you can.

Now let's look at the core competencies required for a GCHQ intelligence analyst:

Teamwork

The first core competency is teamwork. Teamwork is extremely important for a GCHQ intelligence analyst. The reason for this is that as an intelligence analyst, you will be working with a range of other specialists in order to achieve your goals. Not only will you be working with other specialist units in GCHQ, such as engineers or cryptographers, but you will also be working in conjunction with other connected agencies, such as MI5 or MI6.

Keeping the nation secure is not a one man job. It takes the collective effort of every single UK security agency, and as an employee of GCHQ, you will be an integral cog in this machine. This is why it's important that you can work coherently as part of a team, and not just as an individual.

Good teamwork involves the following traits:

- An ability to work through disagreements in a constructive manner.

- An ability to see things from other people's point of view.

- An ability to accept that you are wrong/accept constructive criticism.

- An ability to stand by your own decisions when you know that you are right.

- An ability to put aside your own goals for the good of the team effort.

Leadership and Decision Making

Leadership and decision making is fundamental for GCHQ employees. Leadership doesn't just mean managing other people. It also expands to managing yourself and taking the initiative in difficult situations. Working for GCHQ is not easy. There will be times when you are placed under extreme pressure, and your decisions could have a huge impact on the safety of British citizens. You will need great personal awareness in order to be a good leader.

Good leadership and decision making involves the following traits:

- An ability to help others improve their own weaknesses, in a constructive manner.

- An ability to recognise your own weaknesses, and work to improve them.

- An ability to manage other people, and make key

decisions, so that they can work in an efficient and productive manner.

• An ability to manage yourself, so that you work in an efficient and productive manner.

• An ability to take control and make decisions in difficult situations, to garner fantastic results.

Analytical Skills

In terms of practical skill, this is the number one skill that an intelligence analyst will need in order to succeed at GCHQ. Analytical skills are not something that everyone has, and therefore it's really important that you can demonstrate this effectively during your application. Only the most elite candidates will be chosen to work for GCHQ, and you can expect your analysis skills to be tested to their very limits during the selection process.

So, what do analysis skills involve? When working for GCHQ, your analysis skills will be used to:

• Construct intelligence reports, which can be used to identify potential targets.

• Collate and build up catalogues of intelligence/evidence.

• Deliver learned information in the form of reports and presentations to senior management and government officials, not just from GCHQ but from other agencies such as MI5 or MI6.

• Using data interpretation skills and behavioural analysis

to identify potential threats/targets.

- Intercept and analyse communications between potential threats.

Communication

Communication is another essential competency for GCHQ intelligence analysts. This goes hand-in-hand with teamwork. In order to work as part of the wider GCHQ team, you will need to be an effective communicator, who is capable of conveying your ideas and opinions to a wide range of different people.

As with the other competencies on this list, this is not limited to just those working at GCHQ alongside you, but extends to workers from outside agencies, as well as members of the public. Remember that good communication can often be the difference between the success and failure of an operation. When working in intelligence, failure can have disastrous consequences, and therefore it's essential that you can put this competency into practice.

Good communication involves the following traits:

- Recognising verbal cues and body language.

- Understanding how to put your ideas across in a clear, verbal manner.

- Being able to communicate and get along with a wide variety of people, from other cultures and backgrounds.

- Being able to communicate your ideas and thoughts clearly in writing, as well as in person.

Problem Solving

The next core competency that you will need in order to work for GCHQ, is problem solving. Problem solving is incredibly important for GCHQ intelligence analysts, who must be able to think and react quickly to difficult situations. When working for GCHQ, you will be faced with a wide range of different and complex scenarios, all of which will require a quick mind and a high level of problem solving. You will have to use all of the information at your disposal, however limited, to come to safe decisions which will benefit the security of the nation.

Problem solving involves the following traits:

- Being able to produce creative resolutions to problems.

- Being able to think on your feet and react well to unexpected scenarios.

- Being able to adapt your methods and solutions in order to deal with evolving situations.

Honesty and Integrity

While this is not necessarily a skill, it is still a fundamental quality that you must possess in order to work for GCHQ. Given that you are working in one of the most integral national security agencies in the country, it goes without saying that GCHQ need to be able to trust you. With this in mind, if there is anything in your personal or professional history that suggests that you aren't trustworthy, you are highly unlikely to be selected.

Honesty and integrity involves the following traits:

- Being able to keep your job role secret, from everyone but your closest family.

- Not disclosing any of the information that you have learned whilst working at GCHQ with anyone outside of the organisation/those you are working with.

- Having a full understanding of why secrecy is important to an organisation such as GCHQ.

- Taking a mature approach to your work and your colleagues, putting aside any personal differences in a professional manner.

Now that we've looked at what a GCHQ intelligence analyst does, and what qualities you will need to succeed, it's time to prepare for the application process.

CHAPTER 2

GCHQ Application

Form

The very first stage of the GCHQ selection process is the application questionnaire. This is an online application form, which also doubles as a vetting questionnaire. In short, it's a great way for GCHQ to a) make sure that you match up to their qualifications, and b) make sure you meet their eligibility requirements. Along with the application form, you will also be required to submit a CV. In chapter 3, we will provide you with a full breakdown of the best way to do this.

The application form itself is fairly simple to complete. While you will need to fill in extensive personal details, including those of your mother and father, you won't need to complete competency based questions at this stage. The form consists of 4 or 5 pages, and therefore it's important that you take your time and check your form over carefully before you submit it. Our advice is to print out the form once you have completed it, and then read over your responses. Keep a spare copy next to you, because you will need it later in the process!

Now, let's go through each stage of the application form, and look at the type of questions you'll be asked to complete.

Stage 1 – Personal Details

Email:

Title:

First name:

Middle name:

Last name:

Previous surnames (if applicable):

National Insurance Number:

Permanent Address

Country:

County:

Town:

House name/number:

Post Code:

Length of time that you have lived at this address:

Home telephone number:

Preferred contact number:

Country of birth:

County of birth:

Town of birth:

Nationality at birth:

At the time of writing, do you have British nationality?

Passport number:

In the past, have you ever had any other nationality than British?

Do you currently hold dual nationality?

Are there any legal restrictions that could prevent you from staying and working in the UK?

In the past 10 years, have you spent any time living outside of the UK (excluding holidays)?

If you answered yes to the previous question, please confirm that you can provide a suitable referee as a reference for this period. All referees must be British nationals and available for interview within the UK.

Stage 2 – Further Questions

Are you a currently serving Civil Servant seeking transfer?

Have you applied for and been rejected from this role within the last year?

Have you ever unsuccessfully applied for any other roles within our organisation?

Do you have any other on-going job applications with us?

Can you confirm that you are happy for us to share your information with our government departments if necessary?

Are you currently or have you ever applied for any other governmental roles/departments?

In the event that your application is unsuccessful, would you be happy for us to consider you for other vacancies, or pass your application over to other governmental agencies?

Stage 3 – Family Details

Father's full name:

Father's date of birth:

Father's full place of birth (town, county and country):

Father's full address:

Date from which your father has lived at this address:

Father's nationality at birth:

Father's current nationality:

Does your father hold dual nationality?

Mother's full name:

Mother's date of birth:

Mother's full place of birth (town, county and country):

Mother's full address:

Date from which your mother has lived at this address:

Mother's nationality at birth:

Mother's current nationality:

Does your mother hold dual nationality?

Do you have a partner?

If yes, you will need to repeat this series of questions for your partner.

Stage 4 – Skills and Further Questions

In order to help us determine your suitability for the role, please select one of the following two options, according to how well it describes your experience:

Strong experience: You will likely have applied to GCHQ after working in a similar role elsewhere, and your qualifications are backed up by a good and relevant degree. You are capable of taking on difficult and challenging pieces of work, and can be relied on to take some degree of initiative in the way that you deal with them.

Significant experience: This is more suited to senior or leadership based roles. You will be someone who already has significant experience of leading teams of people in complex and difficult tasks, and have shown that you are responsible and capable enough to work in a supervisory/ authoritative position. You will have extensive technical skill and knowledge, to back up your leadership abilities.

Stage 5 – Vetting Questionnaire

Today's date:

Your date of birth:

Have you ever been found guilty/convicted of a criminal offence in any country (excluding parking offences)?

Have you ever been placed on probation, received a caution, a fixed penalty notice or an Anti-Social Behaviour Order?

Have you ever been conditionally or unconditionally discharged after being charged with committing an offence?

Is there currently a pending court action against you?

Have you ever had any penalty points against your driving license?

Have you ever been subject to disciplinary orders or dismissals from work?

Drugs

GCHQ is fully aware that some of its candidates may have used drugs in the past. This will not usually have any bearing on your application, however you must be completely open about any previous drug use in this section. During the vetting process, you will need to take a drugs test. From the point that you fill in this application, to the time of testing including if you are successful, you must abstain from further use. GCHQ has a no drugs policy.

Have you ever tried, used or experimented with illegal drugs, such as ecstasy or herion?

Have you ever misused or abused prescription drugs or medication?

Have you ever used or experimented with legal highs, such as poppers, or misused solvents?

Have you ever been diagnosed with any of the following: *depression / panic attacks / a mental illness or disorder?*

Have you ever self-harmed or attempted suicide?

Have you ever been made bankrupt or been subject to an IVA (Individual Voluntary Agreement)?

Stage 6 – CV

The final section of your application form will require you to submit a CV and Cover Letter.

In the next chapter, we'll give you some guidance on how to do this.

CHAPTER 3
GCHQ CV

So, you've reached the end of your GCHQ application form, and now you find yourself needing a CV. You might be wondering how to go about constructing this.

In this chapter, we'll show you exactly how to complete the CV to ensure you hit the right notes, and impress the assessors.

What is a CV?

While I'm sure you will be familiar with the basic concept of a CV (Curriculum Vitae), it's important to lay out in clear terms what a CV is. From my experience, far too many people only understand the basic requirements of a CV and not the long term requirements. As a result, their CV is relatively poor and will be looked upon unfavourably by employers.

A CV is essentially a tailored collection of your past achievements, accomplishments and experience. The key word here is **tailored.** One of the biggest mistakes that I see most people make is that they fail to tailor their CV to the employer to whom they are applying. As a result, the person looking at the CV is given a confusing collection of information, most of which they aren't really interested in. The same is true for GCHQ.

While you should be extensive and honest about the places in which you have worked, and the experience you have gained, don't tell them more than they need to know. Keep your experience and history relevant and on topic. For example, GCHQ does not need to know that when you were 16 you worked on a building site for 6 months. They do however need to know that you have experience in analysis,

technological systems and data interpretation – all qualities that make you suitable for this job position.

Another issue that many people have when applying to GCHQ is that because the application form requires you to simply paste in your CV (rather than sending or attaching it as an individual document), they lose all of their formatting. Once you've pasted this in, GCHQ encourage you to spend some time spacing your application out so that it looks presentable. I would strongly recommend you do take the time to do this. Don't be put off by the lack of formatting, as GCHQ won't judge you for this. Just make sure that your CV is formatted clearly.

How to start your CV

When starting a CV, the first step is to list your name, contact number and email address. Be careful when you list your email address. Unprofessional emails, for example, *'SxyJade123@ hotmail.com'* can seriously damage your application. When applying for jobs, it's important to make sure that you use a professional sounding address. The best advice we can give you is to stick to a simple and to the point Gmail address, for example *'JohnSmith1985@gmail.com'*.

Following this, it's time to construct your personal profile. Your personal profile should consist of 1 or 2 paragraphs about you, your interest in the role and your experience. Try to keep this short, relevant and on topic. Remember that this is your chance to introduce yourself as a person to GCHQ, so you need to make yourself sound both professional and interested.

'I am an experienced, analytical and technically gifted individual who is looking for the chance to work within a highly specialised field. I have high GCSE and A Level grades in computer science, and this is a subject that I followed up at degree level and then at Masters, with a postgraduate degree in cybersecurity. I've worked as a cybersecurity analyst for a high profile consulting company for the past 2 years, and this has given me valuable experience in the field.

One of the areas in which I am most interested is fighting the spread of terrorism and crime. I understand that now more than ever before, there is a need for qualified cybersecurity specialists, and that is why I have applied to become an intelligence analyst. I believe that my combination of technical and analytical skills can be invaluable to GCHQ, and I would be very grateful if you would consider my application'.

Academic Achievements

The next step is to list your grades and academic achievements. This should be laid out as clearly as possible. You should start with your most recent academic accomplishments, and then work backwards.

Take note of our earlier advice: try not to make this section too bloated. GCHQ do not need to know every single GCSE that you have, nor anything beyond that. Stick with the main academic achievements, which are mostly postgraduate, degree and A Level. For example:

Academic Achievements:

Ficshire University

Master's Degree in Cybersecurity – First Class Honours, 2011

Bachelor's Degree in Computer Science – 2:1, 2009

Ficshire Grammar School

A Level Computer Science – A*, 2008

A Level Mathematics – A, 2008

A Level Physics – B, 2008

A Level English Literature – A, 2008.

GCSE Physics, Maths, Chemistry and Computer Science, A*. Further high GCSE's in English, General Studies and Design.

Work Experience

The next stage is to fill out your work experience/job history. This is an extremely important stage, and therefore it's important that you get this right. GCHQ will give great credence to candidates who can demonstrate that they have already performed similar job related tasks.

Given the nature of the role, you can see how experience would be highly valuable to GCHQ. You should take the same approach to your job history as you did with your education. Make sure that there are no unexplained gaps, but only provide essential detail on the most important roles. For example:

Cybersecurity Consultant, Ficshire LTD. 2013-2015.

Tasks included: monitoring company network and firewall, consulting with clients over perceived threats and weaknesses to their business network, helping clients deal with ongoing threats to their business network, leading large teams in 'clean-up' operations for business clients, training new staff members and client staff in dealing with cyber threats.

Cybersecurity Analyst, Ficshire Inc. 2011-2013.

Tasks included: working as a member of a team of cybersecurity analysts, training with senior staff members to reach required levels, giving presentations at team meetings, consulting with company clients, filing monthly progress reports based on personal progress, using InTAX software to secure company servers and monitor firewall.

Customer Services Assistant/Telephone Operator, Ficshire Express. 2010-2011.

Part time role whilst studying at University. Tasks included: working on supermarket/shop floor dealing with customers, answering telephones, training new staff members, working the customer help desk and assisting with advertising/sales campaigns.

Key Skills

Next, it's time to summarise your key skills. This section is really important, as it is designed to show GCHQ that you have the skills they are looking for, in an easy to read format. Buzz words such as *experienced, capable, expert,*

constructive, analytical, hard-working, professional etc are all great to use in this section. However, try to keep it short and to the point. For example:

- **Experienced** team leader and team player, **capable** of working **constructively** with anyone else in the unit.

- **Excellent** communicator, **capable** of presenting and conveying ideas to a wide range of people.

- A **fantastic** knowledge of a wide range of ICT based systems, **expert** knowledge in almost all big anti-virus software packages, **expert** knowledge on firewall systems and ICT security procedures.

- **Superb** analytical skills, able to take initiative and make well thought out judgements on difficult scenarios.

- An **expert** knowledge, understanding and experience of dealing with online threats, tracking criminal activity and providing **excellent** solutions to potential security risks.

<u>Hobbies and Interests</u>

The penultimate stage of your CV is to talk about your hobbies and interests. This section is more important than most people believe it to be, but not in the way that you might think.

Really, the hobbies and interests section of your CV is more about what you don't say, than what you do say. It's best to keep this section very brief and relevant to the topic. You need to try and show that you are a liberal person without any offensive hobbies. Steer clear of anything controversial,

and keep it to one paragraph or less. Ideally you should use this section to convey an interest in the subject at hand, for example – computer science.

Now that you've seen how to construct your CV, it's time for another puzzle! Take a look at the question below, and see if you can work out the answer:

GCHQ Brain Teaser, Exercise 2

After a local robbery, five suspects were being interviewed by the investigative bodies.

Eventually the detectives managed to get a confession out of the men. Below is a summary of their statements and it turns out that exactly 5 of these statements were true.

Using the statements, try and work out who committed the crime.

Brian said:

It wasn't Jason

It was Ronald

Jason said:

It wasn't Brian

It was Nathan

Ronald said:

It wasn't Nathan

It wasn't Jason

Nathan said:

It wasn't Martin

It was Brian

Martin said:

It wasn't Ronald

It was Nathan

Clue: How many statements would be true if Brian was the culprit?

Answer: Martin committed the crime.

Based on the clue, if we assume Brian was the person who did it, there would be 6 true statements. This means that it can't be Brian. If you repeat this process for all 5 suspects, the only way that all 5 statements could be true was if Martin was the perpetrator.

CHAPTER 4

GCHQ Online Test

The next stage of the process is an online test. The purpose of this test is to act as a sifting mechanism, to filter out unsuitable candidates from the process. Working for GCHQ is a very popular choice of career, but unfortunately only the most elite candidates are selected. This means that by the time they arrive at this point, GCHQ have a huge number of candidates to sort through. One of the best and most efficient ways to determine the strongest candidates from the weakest, is via an online sifting test.

What type of test will I have to take?

The format of the GCHQ online test will differ between years, and in some years you may not need to take one at all, but if you do have to take the test then you can assume that it will be extremely challenging. There are three different types of test that you might be required to take. These tests are:

- *Situational Judgement*

- *Verbal Reasoning*

- *Numerical Reasoning*

In this section, we will give you a detailed insight into what all of these tests entail, and what their results show. The Verbal and Numerical Reasoning tests will also prove good practice, as you are highly likely to face at least one or both of these assessment types during the GCHQ assessment centre.

Situational Judgement Tests

A situational judgement test is a written/online multiple-choice assessment, which is designed to determine how you react in certain situations. As you might have guessed, the test examines your ability to *judge* a situation, and then make good decisions based on the information that you have been presented with. There are technically no right or wrong answers in a situational judgement test, but there are answers which match with the GCHQ values and behavioural expectations.

While you should be completely honest in your responses, it's important that before answering, you think about how your response will come across to the assessors. The test will examine factors such as how reasonable you are in certain situations, your tolerance, your capacity for self-improvement, your patience and your ability to deal with other people.

One mistake that many people make, is that they overlook the importance of this test. As we mentioned earlier, it's essential that GCHQ know you are someone with honesty and integrity, who can act in a professional manner. With this in mind, let's take a look at a simple situational judgement type question, which is similar to what you might be asked in the exam.

Sample Question

You are working on the customer services desk of a shop floor, when an angry customer approaches. She is holding the hand of her 4 year old son. She tells you that one of the shop assistants shouted at her son for misbehaving, and that he is very upset. After you have finished listening to the woman's side of the story, her son throws his sticky lollipop at you, which gets tangled in your hair. The woman does not seem bothered.

How would you deal with this?

A – Tell the woman in no uncertain terms that she needs to control her child, and that she should think twice about bringing him into this shop again.

B – Tell the woman that you will inform the store manager about your colleague's behaviour.

C – Apologise, and offer the child a replacement lollipop.

D – Apologise for your colleague's behaviour, but tell the woman that she should not allow her son to misbehave whilst on the premises.

E – Shout at the boy, and demand that he apologises for throwing his lollipop at you. Throw the lollipop back.

So, which option should you choose? Let's look in more detail at the responses:

A – Tell the woman in no uncertain terms that she needs to control her child, and that she should think twice about bringing him into this shop again.

This response is assertive, but also misplaced. You have no right to tell the customer that she shouldn't bring her child into the shop; and risk losing her custom for good. It does not take into account the stress that the woman might be under.

B – Tell the woman that you will inform the store manager about your colleague's behaviour.

This response pins all of the blame on your colleague, and excuses the child's behaviour, leaving him free to behave like this in the store in future.

C – Apologise, and offer the child a replacement lollipop.

See 'Option B' for same explanation.

D – Apologise for your colleague's behaviour, but tell the woman that she should not allow her son to misbehave whilst on the premises.

This is a good response, as it is assertive without being insulting. It ensures that the customer feels valued, but also lays down a firm marker in regards to the boy's unacceptable

behaviour.

E – Shout at the boy, and demand that he apologises for throwing his lollipop at you. Throw the lollipop back.

This response is highly unprofessional, and makes you look immature.

As you might have guessed, the best answer to this question is option D. It's a professional, assertive and diplomatic response, which takes into account both the value of the customer and the behavioural expectations of the store. It shows that you are someone who can be relied upon to behave in this manner in real life. For GCHQ, that is an essential quality.

<u>Verbal Reasoning</u>

The second test that you might be asked to take, is a Verbal Reasoning test. A Verbal Reasoning test will assess how well you can ascertain key information, from large passages of text. The questions will require you to draw logical or inarguable conclusions from the passage. With this in mind, it's important to remember that you must base your answers **only** on the information from the passage you have been given. For example, if you were asked a question based on a passage that is pro something you disagree with, you must not let your personal opinions impact upon the answer. Do not rely on any previous knowledge or personal experiences with the subject, as this could easily lead you to the wrong conclusion.

The key to Verbal Reasoning is to make sure you read the whole passage carefully, before you begin the process of gleaning key information from the text. Both of these elements are extremely important if you wish to succeed. Firstly, it's essential that you read the whole passage, in order to get a good idea of the author's argument, and the tone of their work. Secondly, it's important that you can work with speed and precision. The online test will be a timed exercise, and while the time limit won't be too strict, it is designed to put you under pressure. Therefore it's imperative that you can answer the questions in an efficient manner.

Let's look at a sample verbal reasoning question, to give you an idea of what to expect.

Sample Question

Passage - Diving In Football

Speaker A – Diving (or flopping as it's known in the USA) is the practice of faking or exaggerating injury in football, in order to con or cheat the referee – thereby gaining an advantage. Whether that advantage is a free kick or a penalty, the result is irrelevant. The bottom line is that this has to stop. The phrase 'football is a man's game' is horrendously outdated, but there is some truth behind it. Not only is diving cheating, but it slows the game down. It's embarrassing to watch perfectly healthy athletes pretending to be hurt, and it's even worse when your team suffers the consequences of it. Cheating is cheating, plain and simple. We need to kick this out of the game, before it kills football altogether.

Speaker B – One of the biggest debates currently raging in football at the moment, particularly in the United Kingdom, is on the issue of diving. Speak to almost any football fan in the UK about the subject of diving, and you'll be met with anger, rage and frustration. You'll hear phrases such as 'football is a man's game' and 'diving is cheating'. Britain's rage towards diving is palpable. More so than any other country, Britain holds the moral integrity of its footballers above all else. The ideal British footballer is strong, quick and above all else – honest. Unfortunately, the bottom line is that this image just isn't not true.

Question 1. What is the overall point that Speaker A is trying to make?

A – Diving is not manly.

B – Diving is embarrassing.

C – Diving is outdated.

D – Diving needs to be stopped.

Answer: D

Explanation: When answering this type of question, look at the speaker's overall argument. While the speaker does mention the first two points, they are both used as part of his wider overall argument that diving needs to be stopped.

Question 2. In paragraph 2, speaker A uses the term 'bottom line'. What is the name for this type of phrase?

A – Idiomatic

B – Platonic

C – Idiosyncratic

D – Nomothetic

Answer: A

Explanation: The term bottom line is being used here as an idiomatic expression, otherwise known as a phrase that is distinctive to the language or dialect from which it comes.

Numerical Reasoning

The final online test that you might be required to take, is a Numerical Reasoning test. A Numerical Reasoning test is designed to assess mathematical knowledge through number-related assessments. These assessments can be of different difficulty levels, and will all vary depending at which stage of the process you are taking the test. For the purposes of the GCHQ online test, you can expect the questions to be based at an intermediate level. Once you reach the assessment centre stage of the process, you can expect to take harder Numerical Reasoning questions.

Numerical Reasoning tests cover a wide range of mathematical formulae, so it is imperative that you have practiced as much as you can before taking this test. If you are unfamiliar with the concepts involved, it is very likely that you will struggle, and fail the assessment. In order to pass a Numerical Reasoning test, you will need to be proficient in areas such as:

- Adding and subtracting.

- Fractions, percentages and decimals.

- Areas and perimeters.

- Data analysis.

- Mean, Mode, Median and Range.

Along with the above areas, you will also be asked questions on topics such as ratio, time, number sequences, multiplication and division.

Now, let's look at a sample numerical reasoning question, to give you an idea of what to expect:

Country	Jan	Feb	Mar	Apr	May	Jun	Total
UK	21	28	15	35	31	20	150
Germany	45	48	52	36	41	40	262
France	32	36	33	28	20	31	180
Brazil	42	41	37	32	35	28	215
Spain	22	26	17	30	24	22	141
Italy	33	35	38	28	29	38	201
Total	195	214	192	189	180	179	1149

Question 1

What percentage of the overall total was sold in April?

A	B	C	D	E
17.8%	17.2%	18.9%	16.4%	21.6%

Question 2

What is the average number of units per month imported to Brazil over the first 4 months of the year?

A	B	C	D	E
28	24	32	38	40

Question 3

What month saw the biggest increase in total sales from the previous month?

A	B	C	D	E
January	February	March	April	May

Answers

Q1. D = 16.4

EXPLANATION = to work out the percentage overall total that was sold in April, divide how many bikes were sold in April (189) by the total (1149) and then multiply it by 100. (189 ÷ 1149 x 100 = 16.4).

Q2. D = 38

EXPLANTATION = to work out the average number of units per month imported to Brazil over the first 4 months of the year, you add up the first 4 amounts (Jan-April) and then divide it by how many numbers there are (4). So, (42 + 41 + 37 + 32 = 152 ÷ 4 = 38).

Q3. B = February

EXPLANATION = to work out the biggest increase in total sales from the previous month, you work out the difference between the totals for each of the month and work out which has the biggest increase. Between January and February, there was an increase by 19. None of the other months have a bigger increase and therefore February is the correct answer.

Now that you've seen an example of each type of question, have a go at our sample tests below. To help you out, we've provided you with a 5 question Situational Judgement test, a 6 question Verbal Reasoning test, and a 5 question Numerical Reasoning test.

Sample Situational Judgement Test

Question 1

You are the project manager of a team of 5. Your group has been tasked with analysing and correlating key intelligence information which has been passed on to you by another sector, before sending it off to MI5. Halfway through the project, one of your team members approaches you, claiming that she no longer wants to work with another member of the team. The reason for this is that she believes the person in question stole her sandwich. The individual threatening to leave the team is highly experienced and her absence would severely damage the group's chances of success. What do you do?

A – Tell the woman that she is being childish and that she should get back to work.

B – Immediately dismiss the accused team member from the group.

C – Ask the other members of your group to intervene.

D – Sit both team members down in a private room to discuss their differences, with the aim of keeping the group together.

E – Tell the woman that you will buy her a replacement sandwich.

Question 2

You are the temporary manager of a clothing shop. The general manager is out for the day, and has left you in charge. The day in question is 22nd December, and therefore the store is extremely busy with Christmas shoppers. 3 hours before closing time, at the busiest time of the day, the fire alarm goes off. There have been several false alarms in the past, and your staff believe this to be no different. They tell you not to evacuate the store, as this will make the customers angry, and cost the company money. What do you do?

A – Get everyone out of the store safely, and call the fire service to deal with the situation.

B – Call the fire service, but remain with the customers and staff inside the store.

C – Ignore the alarm, it will stop soon anyway.

D – Evacuate the customers from the store, but remain inside to ensure that no damage is done to the stock.

E – Call your manager on their mobile to ask what you should do.

Question 3

You are walking through the park when you come across a family of 3. The family consists of a mother, father and a young toddler of about 3 years old. The young child has a cigarette in his mouth, and looks pale in the face. What do you do?

A – Ignore the situation. It is none of your business.

B – Confront the family, demanding to know why a child of that age is smoking.

C – Pull the mother and father to one side, and ask them whether they think it's acceptable for their child to be smoking.

D – Pull up the number for child protection services, and ring them immediately.

E – Ask if you can borrow a lighter.

Question 4

You are a new employee at GCHQ, working on an intelligence project, when you receive a cryptic email from an unrecognised address. The sender claims to have game changing information on the case that you are involved in, but will only disclose it under the condition that you don't tell anyone else in the organisation. What do you do?

A – Ignore the email. If it's that important, they'll contact you again.

B – Email the sender back, agreeing to their demands.

C – Show the message to your manager, they are better placed to deal with it than you.

D – Email the sender back, telling them that it is a criminal offence to withhold such information.

E – Show the message to your co-worker sitting next to you, asking what he thinks you should do.

Question 5

You are a waiter at a restaurant, dealing with customers on a busy Saturday night shift. The kitchen is running behind schedule, and therefore some of the dishes are coming out late. Several customers have been complaining that they are hungry and waiting for their food. As you bring the food to a particularly unhappy table, you trip and one of the main dishes falls onto the floor. The man whose food you have dropped is extremely angry. He stands up and spits on your cheek. What do you do?

A – Walk back to the kitchen, and inform your manager of the situation.

B – Grab the man by his shirt collar and shove him over the table.

C – Tell the man to leave the restaurant immediately.

D – Apologise, and offer to retrieve a replacement dish.

E – Leave the restaurant and call the police.

Sample Verbal Reasoning Test

Passage - Social Networking

Social networking has unquestionably become a global phenomenon, which I believe is having a huge impact on our social world. Social networking sites such as Facebook, MySpace and Twitter have experienced exponential growth during the 21st century, and yet some users remain oblivious to how much their social networking profiles can shape, influence and affect their everyday lives.

Information that is posted on these sites is likely to come back and haunt a person in the future. Just think of a social networking site as a type of "global database". You are posting information, facts about yourself, images etc, into your very own "database"; acting as a log of your personal behaviour for others to view. This is a great concern for many parents, who feel obliged to check how secure their child is whilst they're online. Unfortunately, the problem is that these parents have let their child have too much internet freedom in the first place.

Employers often use these sites as a way of maintaining access to their employees outside of the working environment. Although this can be considered morally wrong, employers can track your profile in order to find controversial issues, sensitive matters or inappropriate misconduct. They do this in order to determine the professionalism of their employees outside of the working environment, and to determine their 'suitability' in relation to their careers.

Question 1. Which of the following best describes the author's attitude to social networking sites?

A – Strongly pessimistic.

B – Discouraged.

C – Guarded.

D – Upset.

E – Highly optimistic.

Question 2. The author implies, but does not state, that…

A – Information online, once secured, poses no risk of substantial harm.

B – Parents should be stricter regarding their child using the internet.

C – Employers should be allowed to use social networking sites as a means of keeping an eye on existing or future employees.

D – Children are responsible for using the internet safely and securely.

E – Information founded online can be used as evidence in court.

Passage - Creative Pedagogy

Creative pedagogy is a concept that derives from both science and art. A creative learner is someone who is able to demonstrate high levels of problem solving, along with imaginative and innovative thinking, all of which are deemed essential qualities in life.

Theorist Jean Piaget and his works on child development and observation highlight the importance of education. His views on child mind-set and development, played a huge role in developing his works on educational theory. He conducted his studies through multiple observations, whilst engaging with activities that helped him to gain an understanding of the different processes involved in the developmental stages of children's learning.

He noted that children's thinking did not develop quickly, nor smoothly. It exposed him to the different stages in the development process whereby children would transition into new ways of thinking. These transitions occurred at different stages of a child's learning development. Piaget's work demonstrates the struggle to implement a developmental strategy that could be used to analyse every child.

Question 3. Which of the following words or phrases best describes a creative learner, in the context of the passage?

A – Intellectual thinker.

B – Highly skilled at drawing and painting.

C – Lateral thinker.

D – Selective thinker.

E – Logical and Analytical thinker.

Question 4. From the author's passage on Jean Piaget and social development, you could assume that individual learners differ from each other by…

A – The stages of development.

B – The progression rate at which children develop.

C – The concepts of which children began to understand.

D – Learning techniques being different for each child.

E – The knowledge and understanding a child has about the social world.

Passages - Teenagers

When they are on the verge of becoming a teenager, you will undoubtedly witness an array of changes in your son or daughter. What once was your innocent and beautiful baby, has now reached the stage of adolescence, and must now begin the 'painful' process of developing into a young man or woman.

Now on the cusp of adolescence, you and your child are about to embark on a great voyage. They will become a metamorphosed silhouette of what once was a child. It will be a bumpy ride that is bound to involve tears, laughter, maturity, naivety and independence. You will unwittingly be the guidepost through every experience, as your child blossoms into a young adult.

You will notice at times that everything you do or say to your 'baby' is wrong. I am not going to sugar-coat it, but no matter how many children you have, this will never get easier. You should expect to deal with plenty of heated debates, arguments, pleas and tantrums.

Question 5. In the context of the passage, the use of the word "metamorphosed" is used to describe…

A – The transformation from a teenager into an adult.

B – The scientific changes of emotional behaviour.

C – The changes of a human's intellectual behaviour.

D – The transformation from a child into a teenager.

E – The scientific discovery of human nature.

Question 6. The author uses the phrase, "I am not going to sugar-coat it", in order to convey that…

A – You cannot hide the difficulties of raising a teenager.

B – Despite the challenges, parenting is a rewarding feeling.

C – Parenting is a challenging task and should not be taken lightly.

D – Parenting comes with a great deal of responsibility.

E – Teenagers make it their job to be challenging for their parents.

Sample Numerical Reasoning Test

Question 1

What is the volume of this object?

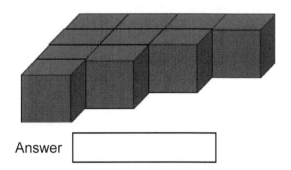

Answer [   ]

Question 2

What is 2⁄8 x 9? Simplify your answer and write it as a mixed fraction.

A	B	C	D
2 1⁄3	1 1⁄4	2 2⁄6	2 1⁄4

Question 3

What is the prime factorisation of 9?

A	B	C	D
3	3 x 9	3 x 3	3 x 3 x 3

Question 4

Among the respondents, 80% of the people who said they walk to school and 90% of the people who said they bike to school also said that their school was less than 5 miles away.

How many people said that they walk or bike to school because it is less than 5 miles away?

Responses when asked how they get to school

A	B	C	D	E
83	97	85	49	71

Question 5

Two of the numbers move from Box A to Box B. The total of the numbers in Box B is now four times the total of the numbers in Box A. Which two numbers move?

Box A

2   6

3

9

4

Box B

10   1

7

8

5

Answer [   ]

Answers to Situational Judgement

1. D. Sit both team members down in a private room to discuss their differences, with the aim of keeping the group together.

Explanation: This is the most reasonable and liberal approach to the situation, and ensures that you have made your best attempt to keep the team working together in a smooth fashion.

2. A. Get everyone out of the store safely, and call the fire service to deal with the situation.

Explanation: This is a no brainer. In order to meet with health and safety regulations, it's essential that you evacuate in the event of a fire drill, regardless of whether staff and customers like it.

3. C. Pull the mother and father to one side, and ask them whether they think it's acceptable for their child to be smoking.

Explanation: This is the most reasonable approach to the situation. Unless you have solid evidence that the child has been given the cigarette by his parents, you cannot report this as a crime. However, you can raise your concerns about the situation in a calm and reasonable fashion.

4. C. Show the message to your manager, they are better placed to deal with it than you.

Explanation: This is the most logical approach to the situation. The fact that you are a new employee may have an impact on your decision, but really it doesn't make a difference unless you are in a management position. The email could be legitimate, in which case it needs to be looked at by those

better placed than you. Part of good decision making is knowing when to pass the responsibility on to someone else.

5. A. Walk back to the kitchen, and inform your manager of the situation.

> **Explanation:** *This is the most reasonable approach to the situation. Although you will obviously be upset and extremely angry at the situation, taking it into your own hands will make things worse. You should inform your manager, who will take the necessary steps to remove the man from the restaurant and inform the authorities. Spitting is regarded as assault, which is a criminal offence.*

Answers to Verbal Reasoning

1. C. Guarded.

> **Explanation:** *Guarded is the best word from the list, which fits with the author's attitude. The main point that the author is trying to make is that children need to be more careful about what they post on social networking sites, as it could come back to hurt them in the long term. Therefore, the author encourages caution.*

2. D. Parents should be stricter regarding their child using the internet.

> **Explanation:** *Answer option D is the only option that is implied, and not directly stated. The author makes specific mention to the fact that some parents 'have let their child have too much internet freedom in the first place', heavily implying that they need to be stricter.*

how2become

3. C. Lateral thinker.

Explanation: The term "lateral thinker" best describes the author's perception of a critical learner. The passage clearly indicates that creativity and imagination are crucial for a child's development in regards to creative pedagogy. The use of the word "lateral" refers to imagination and innovation, and therefore best describes a person with a creative mind.

4. B. The progression rate at which children develop.

Explanation: You could assume from the passage that individual learners differ from one another because of "the progression rate at which children develop". Piaget emphasises how children adapt to situations at various stages of their life. This suggests that children do not develop at the same pace.

5. D. The transformation from a child into a teenager.

Explanation: The use of the word "metamorphosed" is used to highlight "the transformation from a child into a teenager". The passage specifically discusses the changes children face when dealing with the struggles of adolescence, and therefore illustrates how these changes modify the way we see a child, who is on the verge of 'growing up'.

6. A. You cannot hide the difficulties of raising a teenager.

Explanation: The author uses the phrase, "I am not going to sugar-coat it" in order to convey that "you cannot hide the difficulties of raising a teenager". The author states the complexities of raising a teenager throughout the passage, thereby illustrating that they are not hiding away from the truths, despite how unappealing they may be.

Answers to Numerical Reasoning

1. B. 10 cubic units

Explanation: As you will notice, the diagram shows 10 blocks, therefore the volume of the shape will have to be 10 cubic units.

2. D. 2 ¼

Explanation: This may seem tricky, but you must remember that '9' is also a fraction. You need to add the 1 underneath it to make 9⁄1.

So, 9⁄1 x 2⁄8 = 9 x 2 = 18 and 1 x 8 = 8. This gives us the fraction = 18⁄8. This can be simplified to 9⁄4 and as a mixed fraction, is equivalent to = 2 1⁄4.

3. C. 3 x 3

Explanation: You need to work out which answer option includes prime numbers that are also factors of 9.

3 is a prime number, the question is, how do we get from 3 to 9, still using only prime numbers? 3 x 3 = 9 and therefore contains factors of 9, which are still prime numbers.

4. B. 97

Explanation: First you need to work out the percentage of the people who walked = 80% of 65 = 65 ÷ 100 x 80 = 52.

Now, you need to work out the percentage of the people who biked = 90% of 50 = 50 ÷ 100 x 90 = 45.

So, 52 + 45 = 97

5. 4 and 9

Explanation: *If you move 9 and 4 from Box A that leaves the total of:*

6 + 3 + 2 = 11

If you add the 9 and 4 to Box B, you will get a total of:

9 + 4 + 10 + 1 + 7 + 5 + 8 = 44

Therefore the total of box B is now four times bigger than box A.

CHAPTER 5

GCHQ Telephone

Interview

The next stage of the selection process is a telephone interview. Just as with the online tests, there is some flexibility in whether you will have to take this or not. You should check with GCHQ before the selection process in order to find out whether you should prepare for a telephone interview.

If you do have to take a telephone interview, then this chapter will prepare you with some fantastic tips on how to impress the GCHQ assessor.

What is the GCHQ telephone interview?

A telephone interview is an interview that takes place, as you guessed it, over the phone. In GCHQ's case, this is a telephone interview that lasts around 30 minutes. It will usually take place with someone from a management position in the company. You might be questioned on everything from your basic skillset/knowledge of GCHQ, to your motivations for applying to the organisation.

How do I prepare for the GCHQ telephone interview?

As we have mentioned, in order to pass the GCHQ telephone interview, you will need to prepare extremely thoroughly. Often, the telephone interview stage is simply used as a filtering mechanism, particularly when there are a high volume of candidates for the position.

You will have already been through 2 sifting phases in order to reach this stage, with the next step being the assessment centre. This means that while your competition for the role will get smaller after each stage of the process, the standard of that competition will only get higher, and you'll be tested to

your limits.

There are a number of ways that you can prepare for the telephone interview, but arguably the most important advice that we can provide you is to **learn your CV.**

The person interviewing you will have a copy of your CV and application form next to them whilst speaking to you. While it's possible for you to have the same documents in front of you (and you absolutely should!) it will detract from your ability to interview if you are rifling through different pieces of paper trying to find an answer, whilst still speaking to the interviewer. The better you know your own qualifications and experience, the more confident you will come across to the person on the other end of the phone.

The next thing you need to do to prepare for the phone interview is to **learn as much as you can about the role**. Naturally, the interviewer will be asking you questions about how much you know and how interested you are. Therefore it's imperative that you can demonstrate prior knowledge, and consequently enthusiasm. While you shouldn't expect to be grilled continuously on how much you know about the company, the interviewer will expect you to have conducted thorough prior research about both GCHQ, and the role you are applying for. The more knowledge you can demonstrate, the better your chances of getting the job.

Another thing that you can do to improve your chances, is to **prepare your environment**. For some people this might seem trivial, however it's actually extremely important. When taking any telephone interview, you need to make sure that it's

done in a calm and relaxing environment, without background noise, interruptions or distractions. Not only will this allow you to hear the interviewer properly, but it will also help you to focus on your own responses, and conduct the interview with as little stress as possible.

Finally, the other thing that you must have next to you is a copy of the **job specification.** When you applied for the job, you should have read through the description advertised thoroughly, before deciding that it was what you wanted to do. Have this to hand, because you will be questioned on it.

Sample Intelligence Analyst:

Job Specification

For the purposes of this exercise, let's take a look at a real life sample intelligence analyst job advert.

Intelligence Analyst:

Basic Salary - £25,500

Location – Cheltenham

Job Description

While working as a GCHQ intelligence analyst, you will be responsible for using analytical and digital skills to interpret complex and technical data, with the aim of helping to protect the UK from internal and external threats.

Your role

GCHQ are responsible for gathering essential intelligence information from around the world, and putting this information to good use in the fight against cybercrime, terrorism and other criminal activities. As a GCHQ intelligence analyst, you will be tasked with interpreting essential information, in order to produce critical intelligence material.

The role of an intelligence analyst is extremely challenging and complex, but is hugely exciting. Your priorities and goals will change according to what is going on in the world at the time, and sometimes you could find yourself taking part in projects lasting several months or even years. It is your job to come to key decisions on the value of intelligence, and create critical reports based on your discoveries.

Job requirements

In order to qualify for this role, you will need:

- A minimum 2:2 degree, in any subject.

- An up-to-date knowledge and interest in current affairs, and new technology.

- An ability to write fluently and communicate effectively in written form.

- Developed and demonstrable analytical skills.

- The ability to tackle large sets of data in an efficient manner, if and when required.

Full training will be provided to successful applicants. GCHQ have a developed training programme in place to ensure that

their intelligence analysts become essential components in the security of the United Kingdom.

How to break down a job description

When looking at any job description, it's integral that you are able to break down the information provided into smaller details, in order for you to analyse exactly what you need to do to succeed. Let's start from the beginning of the job description, and work our way down:

'You will be responsible for using analytical and digital skills to interpret complex and technical data.'

Right from the start, the job description makes reference to one of the core competencies. Analytical skills are integral for any GCHQ intelligence analyst. Note this down, as you will need to use it during your telephone interview answers.

'The aim of helping to protect the UK from internal and external threats.'

In order to work for GCHQ, it's essential that you can show them how much you care. It allows you to build your responses to motivational type questions, such as why you want the role in the first place. Of course, I am not suggesting you lie. If you don't care about helping to protect the UK, then you shouldn't be working at an organisation such as GCHQ. The job description tells you that they want people who care for their cause, and not just someone looking to take home a pay check. Successful candidates won't just be talented, they will be motivated to make a difference too.

'Your priorities and goals will change according to what is going on in the world at the time.'

This is the next line that should draw your attention. If you are looking to apply for a job where the work is exactly the same every day, then GCHQ is not for you. In order to work for GCHQ you need to be a highly adaptable person, who is capable of altering their methods and solutions according to the situation. Technology is developing at a breath-taking pace. While this provides you with access to fantastic tools and equipment, which can be used to fight terrorism and crime, it unfortunately means that those same criminals are constantly updating and improving their methods of escaping detection. In order to combat this, GCHQ intelligence analysts need to stay on top of things at all times, and that means updating and improving your methods. You must be a highly flexible person if you want to work for GCHQ.

'An up-to-date knowledge and interest in current affairs.'

This is a really important line, which many people might skip over. It means that during your phone interview, there is a good chance you might be asked questions which require your opinion on issues going on around the world. If you aren't someone who really follows the news, this might seem unfair, and it might catch you off guard, but if it's in the job description, then you need to pay attention to it. As we mentioned, GCHQ want people who care about their cause. You don't have to have an extensive knowledge of world events but if you can hold a conversation with the interviewer and express your opinion, this is a fantastic plus against your name.

'An ability to write fluently and communicate effectively in written form.'

Finally, the job description makes clear reference to your (non-verbal) communication abilities. As we have already explained, this is highly important for a number of reasons. Intelligence analysts will be required to construct clear and detailed reports based on their findings. It's integral that these reports are easily understandable, free from error and make things crystal clear for those reading, because it is on these reports that key intelligence judgements are made. The consequences of a bad or misleading report could be utterly disastrous. During the assessment centre stage, you will be tested heavily on your written abilities.

<u>By looking at the above, we can build up the following profile:</u>

GCHQ are looking for a flexible candidate, with great analytical skills, and a keen knowledge in current affairs and new technology. You must be someone who genuinely cares about protecting the UK from global and internal threats, and have the ability to communicate succinctly in writing.

The reason that this exercise is important is that by breaking down the job description, we ultimately make our lives easier during the telephone interview. The interviewer will have a copy of the description to hand, and will be asking questions based on it. Therefore, by breaking down and determining which qualities are the most important, you can second guess which questions are coming. This makes your preparation for the phone interview much easier, and consequently improves your chances of passing.

Now, let's have a look at some sample telephone interview questions, and how to answer them. Later in this guide, I will give you a full and extensive list of interview answers that can be used in the face to face interview. Many of those tips will be useful for this section, too.

Sample Telephone Interview Questions

Q. *'Tell me a bit more about yourself.'*

This is very common telephone interview starter, as it gives the interviewer a chance to gain a personal insight into who you are as a person, and an opportunity to build a rapport with you from the off. Be careful though, the interviewer doesn't want to know everything about your life. Your answer to this question should consist of very short facts about yourself, for example:

'I am 23 years old and studied at South Kent University. I have a degree in Astrophysics, and have worked at Ficshire Community Centre for the last 3 years. Now I'd like the chance to put my experience and expertise to good use. I see GCHQ as the perfect fit for me.'

Q. *'What is it that makes you think that you would be a good fit for GCHQ?'*

This question is an excellent chance for you to show that you have carefully studied the job description (and the organisation) before arriving at this stage. Using the points we listed in the exercise above, you can start to build a case for yourself right from the off:

'I'm a flexible person with great analytical ability, and have demonstrated this on numerous occasions throughout my

career. I believe that my values and those of GCHQ are highly similar. I'm someone who genuinely cares about making a difference in the world, and the UK is at the very centre of my interests. I want to make this a safe country to live in, without the threat from global and internal threats. Working at GCHQ would provide me with a fantastic opportunity to make a difference in this regard. I'm also a keen writer, who has published his thoughts on current global issues via a number of different online channels.'

Q. 'During the process of applying for this job, is there anything you have learned about GCHQ that has surprised you?'

This is a fairly unusual question, but one that you should definitely be prepared for. Although the interviewer will be trying to build a rapport in order to get to know you better, they also want to try to catch you out and see how well you think on your feet. The majority of people won't have prepared for a question like this, and therefore it's an ideal question to ask. Always make sure that your response to this question is positive. For example:

'Yes, there was actually. I had an in-depth knowledge of GCHQ and the way in which they work prior to application, and have learned a great deal more through my research, but I was surprised to learn about the sheer scope of GCHQ operations. Prior to researching, I had no idea that GCHQ had such a major impact on not just British security, but globally too. I learned that in the last year, GCHQ have prevented 7 attacks from occurring on British soil. This was really inspiring to me, and has strengthened my resolve to join your organisation.'

Q. As you'll be aware, the role that you have applied for involves tremendous analytical prowess. Can you give me an example of a time when you have demonstrated your analytical skills?

This is a question that you will probably hear during both the telephone interview, and the face to face interview, so you need to be prepared for it. Generally the telephone interviewer will be using their time to try to get to know you and your interests better, rather than establishing your competencies, but you should always expect to be asked at least one competency based question.

In chapter 7 of this guide, we'll provide you with a complete, in-depth explanation to show you how to respond to this question.

Q. What would you say is your biggest weakness?

This is a tricky question that a lot of candidates slip up on, and is another one that you should expect to hear during the first two interviews.

The answer that you should NOT give to this question, is 'I have no weaknesses'. This will come across badly to the interviewer. The trick to answering this question is to turn your weakness into a positive. Think of something more unique, and honest, such as the fact that you get nervous speaking in front of large groups of people, or that you are a perfectionist.

Everyone has assets that can be improved. GCHQ want someone who is willing to learn and grow as they progress through the company.

In chapter 7 of this guide, we'll provide you with a complete,

in-depth explanation to show you how to respond to this question.

Q. How well do you cope with working as part of a team?

This is another popular question. Ordinarily, during the face to face interviews, you'll be asked to give specific examples of when you have worked as part of a team. In the telephone interview, the assessor will simply be trying to establish your qualities. Therefore while you don't need to give an in-depth example, it is a good idea to provide a broader example in answer to this question.

Remember that teamwork is essential at GCHQ, and you can even use this knowledge in your response. For example:

'I would say that I am an excellent team member. I've worked in teams for most of my career, and I get along with pretty much everyone that I meet. Not only am I a great team member, but I am also a great team leader. I have of wealth of experience in helping my teams to achieve their goals, and I feel that my previous customer service position at Ficshire Service Centre demonstrated this. The team under my leadership won several company based awards for outstanding performance, which I was extremely proud of. I understand how to motivate, communicate and work with others to achieve great things.

From my research, I've learned that teamwork is really important for GCHQ, and I believe my team working skills make me a perfect match for your organisation.'

Other questions that you might be asked in the GCHQ telephone interview include:

- What is your biggest strength?

- What is the one thing that makes working for us the most appealing to you?

- Would you say that you are a flexible person?

- How well do you handle criticism?

- How well do you think your qualifications and career have prepared you for a career in GCHQ?

In chapter 7 of this guide, we have provided you with a comprehensive overview of the GCHQ interview process, including fantastic sample responses to the type of questions you'll be asked, and tips on all of the above.

Before we move on to the next stage, here are some top tips on how to pass YOUR telephone interview.

GCHQ Telephone Interview: 4 Golden Tips

1. Find a quiet place

There is nothing worse than being on the phone to someone that you can barely hear, especially if that person is trying to determine your suitability for a position in their company. Once you find out the time at which the interviewer will ring you, make sure that you find a quiet place to take the call. That means a room without any TV on in the background, people walking in disturbing you or other distractions. It's imperative that you can sit down and focus on what the interviewer is saying.

2. Have your paperwork to hand

The person interviewing you on the telephone will have a copy of your CV, the job description and your application form next to them whilst doing so. This means that you also need to have these 3 items to hand.

Although you should make a sustained effort to learn the things that you have written beforehand, having the paperwork next to you will really help if you ever need to cross reference your qualifications or a particular date/year with the interviewer. There are few things worse than awkward pauses in conversation whilst you try to remember a certain thing.

3. Don't underestimate body language

For most people, body language during a telephone interview doesn't make the slightest bit of a difference. They don't consider how the way they are physically reacting impacts

upon the way they sound down the phone, but the reality is that it does.

Your aim should be to relax, but don't get too relaxed. You don't want to sound disinterested. The ideal position to be taking an interview in is sitting on a quiet sofa away from distraction. Some people like to pace, but this could result in heavy breathing, which is distracting for the interviewer.

4. Practice questions and answers

Some people don't bother to practice their answers for a telephone interview, because they don't believe that the experience can be replicated. These people are wrong. If you really want to go the extra mile, and ensure that you ace the interview, you can and will prepare.

Stage a mock interview with a friend or family member and have them call you, to see how you sound down the phone. Most people aren't aware of how they sound on the other end of the phone line. If your voice is muffled, mumbling or too quiet, then this could be an issue for the interviewer. You must be able to speak clearly and concisely, and deliver your answers in a confident fashion.

The best way to make yourself confident, is to practice as many interview questions and answers as you can.

In the next chapter, we'll take a look at the GCHQ Assessment Centre.

CHAPTER 6
GCHQ Assessment Centre

If you are successful in passing the telephone interview, you will be invited to attend the next stage of the selection process. This stage is the GCHQ Assessment Centre. This consists of a series of difficult exercises and tasks that you will need to complete, before finally taking both a drugs test and a face to face interview. In this chapter, we'll provide you with a comprehensive overview of how to pass the assessment centre.

What is the GCHQ Assessment Centre?

The GCHQ Assessment Centre will take place at an undisclosed, top secret location. Upon arrival, you will be seated with the other candidates who have made it this far in the process. You will be given instructions as to how the day is going to go. From there, you'll take a series of exercises in order to determine your suitability for the role. These can vary from one year to the next. However, these exercises are likely to include:

- A report writing exercise

- A case study analysis exercise

- A verbal reasoning test

- A numerical reasoning test

- A personality questionnaire

Following the completion of these exercises, you will take both a drugs test, and a face to face competency based interview. If you successfully pass both of these, you'll move onto the final stages – another interview, and GCHQ training.

How can I prepare for the GCHQ Assessment Centre?

Before we begin looking at the exercises, it is important to establish one thing – you MUST prepare for the assessment centre. It goes without saying that if you don't prepare, you will fail, and won't gain your dream career with GCHQ. So, how can you make the best use of your preparation time? Allow me to explain.

The GCHQ Assessment Centre is made up of a series of difficult, but ultimately learnable exercises. When I say learnable, what I mean is that it's entirely possible for you to familiarise yourself with the exercises involved. There are a number of ways to do this, but the best way to guarantee success is through **practice.** The more you practice, the more familiar you will become with answering the type of questions involved.

You might have heard of other employers running similar test centres to this, and you may even have seen examples of the questions that they have been asked. The problem is, these companies are not GCHQ. The GCHQ assessment centre tests are only suitable for the most elite candidates. The Numerical Reasoning questions that you'll be asked in the exam will be at an advanced level, and exercises such as the Report Writing task will require you to think on your feet and come up with creative solutions to problems.

In this chapter, we'll provide you with numerous example questions, to help you do this. However, you should make sure that these are not the only practice you undertake before your assessment centre. Purchase test papers online, research,

practice and practice some more. Make sure you take the practice tests under timed conditions, to replicate the speed at which you'll have to work during the actual assessment.

The other thing that you'll need to do before the assessment day, is to make sure that you have learned the core competencies. These will be extremely important if you want to pass the assessment centre. The main reason for this is that the assessment centre interview is competency based. The interviewers will ask you to recount specific and detailed examples of when you have demonstrated the core competencies, for example: *'Can you tell me about a time when you have used your analytical skills to resolve an issue'*, and you will need to respond accordingly.

With this in mind, it's crucial that you have an understanding of why each competency is important for GCHQ employees, and how it can be used in the workplace. Don't be surprised if the interviewers, either at this stage or the next, also ask you to explain why you think it's important for GCHQ employees to have a certain competency.

In chapter 7, we'll recap the competencies and go over how they can be used in the interview.

Now, let's move onto the assessment centre exercises.

GCHQ Report Writing Exercise

In this section, you will be asked to construct a written report or proposal based upon information provided to you. Your report will require you to come up with solutions to problems discussed in the passage or documentation that you've been given.

This is a really important exercise. It closely mirrors the type of activities that you'll be required to do when working as an intelligence analyst. A central part of an intelligence analyst's role involves writing up in-depth intelligence based reports, detailing their findings and suggested solutions to problems/threats. You'll find yourself completing paperwork on a constant basis, and it's vital that this is filled in correctly. As we have mentioned several times throughout this guide, good written communication is absolutely essential for a GCHQ intelligence analyst. A well written proposal could mean the difference between your solutions to an issue being rejected, or even misunderstood. Misunderstandings in intelligence can have fatal consequences, and that is why your paperwork needs to be clear, concise and readable.

Along with good spelling, sentence structure, grammar and punctuation, your report/proposal needs to show GCHQ that you are someone who can think logically about intelligence based situations, and make good decisions. It is no good constructing a well written report if it doesn't address the issues at hand. The information that you will need to assess can take a wide variety of forms, but the topic will largely be based around a fictional intelligence scenario. Let's take a look at an example.

Sample Report Writing Exercise

You are the customer services officer for a fictitious retail centre. Your manager has asked you to compile a report based on a new pub that is being opened at the centre. He is meeting with the pub owners in a few days' time to discuss some issues, and he wants you to write a report based on the information provided. The pub owners have requested that the pub is open to serve alcoholic beverages in the centre from 11am to 11pm.

Below you will find a survey sheet, which tells you that the general public and staff are not particularly happy with the idea of a pub being opened in the shopping centre. They are worried about anti-social behavioural problems, littering and rowdiness.

It is your job to create a report for your manager that states the main issues, and details your recommendations.

Survey Sheet

The following information has been taken from a survey that was conducted amongst 100 members of the public who regularly shop at the centre, and 30 employees who work at the centre:

• 60% of the general public and 80% of employees felt that the opening of a pub in the centre would increase littering.

• 80% of the general public and 60% of employees thought that rowdiness in the centre would increase as a result of the pub opening.

• 10% of the general public and 10% of employees thought

that the opening of the pub would be a good idea.

On the next page, we have provided you with an example of how the report could be constructed. You should consider all of the information from the survey sheet, and make the recommendations that you consider to be the best under the circumstances.

Remember: *recommendations are suggestions for actions or changes. They should be specific rather than general. It is important that you answer the question and state what your main findings and recommendations are.*

<u>Sample response</u>

From: The Customer Services Officer

To: The Centre Manager

Subject: New pub

Dear Sir,

Please find attached a detailed analysis of my findings and recommendations in relation to the pub that is scheduled to be opened in the shopping centre. The survey conducted took into consideration the views and opinions of 100 members of the public, and 30 members of staff who work at the centre.

Whilst a small proportion of the staff and public (10%) felt that the opening of a pub would be a good idea, the majority of people who were surveyed felt that the opening of a pub would lead to problems with anti-social behaviour, rowdiness and littering.

After considering all of the information collected, I would like to make the following recommendations:

The level of customer service that the centre provides is high, and therefore it is important that this is maintained. This cannot be maintained if we do not take into consideration the views and opinions of our customers and staff. I believe that allowing the pub to serve alcohol from 11am till 11pm would pose a significant risk, and could lead to problems with anti-social behaviour. We have a responsibility to protect the public, and to ensure that they are safe whilst in the centre. Whilst it is important to obtain the views of the pub owners, I recommend that for a trial period, the pub is only permitted to serve alcoholic beverages from 11am until 1pm, and from 5pm till 7pm.

Providing there are no problems with anti-social behaviour, littering or rowdiness, then this course of action would allow us to trial the new pub, before re-evaluating its terms. I am prepared to take full responsibility for monitoring the situation once the pub has been opened. I will keep you updated on my progress.

Yours sincerely,

Now that you have read the sample response, take a look at the following 5 step approach that I use when creating a well-structured report.

<u>How to create an effective report</u>

Step 1 – Read the information provided in the exercise quickly and accurately.

Remember that you only have a short time in which to create your report. Therefore, you do not want to spend too long reading the information. I would suggest that you spend 2-3 minutes maximum on this.

Step 2 – Extract relevant information from irrelevant information (main findings).

When you read the information provided in the exercise, you will notice that some of the information is of no significance. Write down which information is relevant in brief details only – these should be your main findings.

Step 3 – Decide what recommendations you are going to suggest or what action(s) you are going to take.

If asked to, then you must come up with suitable recommendations. Do not 'sit on the fence', but provide a logical solution to the problem.

Step 4 – Construct your report in a logical and concise manner.

You are being assessed on your ability to communicate effectively. Therefore you must construct your report in a logical and concise manner. You must also ensure that you answer the question that is being asked.

Step 5 – Include keywords and phrases from the core competencies in your report.

During each report or letter that you construct, I strongly advise that you include keywords and phrases from the core competencies. You will notice that the 5-step approach is easy to follow. Therefore I strongly suggest that you learn and use it during the practice exercises provided later on in this section.

To begin with, let's go back to the sample response that I provided you with in the first exercise. In order to demonstrate what is relevant, I have highlighted the key points from the report.

Key Points

*You are the customer services officer for a fictitious retail centre. Your manager has asked you to compile a report based on a new **pub that is being opened at the centre.** He is meeting with the pub owners in a few days' time to discuss some issues, and he wants you to write a report based on the information provided. **The pub owners have requested that the pub is open to serve alcoholic beverages in the centre from 11am to 11pm.***

*Below you will find a survey sheet, which tells you that the **general public and staff are not particularly happy with the idea** of a pub being opened in the shopping centre. They are worried about antisocial behavioural problems, littering and rowdiness. It is your job to create a report for your manager that **states the main issues**, and details your recommendations.*

<u>So, why are the key points that I have highlighted relevant? Allow me to explain:</u>

'You are the customer services officer'

As a customer services officer, it is your job to provide a high level of service. Therefore the report that you create needs to cater for everyone's needs. In relation to this particular situation, you must provide a solution that caters for the needs of the pub owners, the centre, members of the public and employees.

'New pub that is being opened in the centre'

The information that you have been provided with tells you clearly that a new pub is opening in the centre. The pub is a business, and therefore in order to make money, it needs to serve alcoholic beverages. Bear this in mind when you are detailing your recommendations. The pub owners have quite rightly requested that they are open from 11am till 11pm, and serve alcoholic beverages throughout this period. However, you still need to provide a high level of service to everyone else.

Therefore, you may decide to recommend a reduced opening time, for a trial period only. When constructing a report, always try to look for the obvious solution to the problem. The general public and staff are not happy with the idea of a pub being opened in the shopping centre, therefore you will need to take this into account when constructing your response.

'States what the main issues are'

Your first task when writing your report is to state what your main findings are and what your recommendations would be.

Once you have detailed the main issues, you will then need to make your recommendations based on good judgement and common sense.

During step 3, you will need to come up with your recommendations. Remember that you will need to solve problems based on the information and facts provided. In this particular case, I have decided to offer a solution that meets the needs of all of the parties concerned – reduced opening times for a trial period with a view to extending them if all goes well. When creating your report, do not be afraid to come up with sensible recommendations or solutions.

During step 4, you will create your report. It is important that your report is concise, relevant and flows in a logical sequence. I would strongly recommend that you construct it using the following format:

Beginning:

During the introduction, provide brief details as to what the report is about. You should also provide brief details that relate to your findings. In this particular question I am being asked to detail my main findings and recommendations. I will do this during the beginning section of the report.

Middle:

Here you will write your main findings and recommendations. Remember to include keywords and phrases that you have learnt from the core competencies.

End:

This is the summary and conclusion. Say why you have

recommended this course of action. Are there any further recommendations? If you are expecting feedback, explain how you propose to deal with this. You may also wish to state that you will take full responsibility for seeing any action through, and for keeping your manager updated on progress.

In order to demonstrate how effective this method can be, I have boxed off each section on the following page.

Dear Sir,

Please find attached a detailed analysis of my findings and recommendations in relation to the pub that is scheduled to be opened in the shopping centre. The survey conducted took into consideration the views and opinions of 100 members of the public, and 30 members of staff who work at the centre.

Whilst a small proportion of the staff and public (10%) felt that the opening of a pub would be a good idea, the majority of people who were surveyed felt that the opening of a pub would lead to problems with antisocial behaviour, rowdiness and littering. After considering all of the information collected, I would like to make the following recommendations:

The level of customer service that the centre provides is high, and therefore it is very important that this is maintained. This cannot be maintained if we do not take into consideration the views and opinions of our customers and staff. I believe that allowing the pub to serve alcohol from 11am till 11pm would pose a significant risk, and could (as feared) lead to problems with anti-social behaviour. We have a responsibility to protect the public, and to ensure that they are safe whilst in the centre. While it is important to obtain the views of the pub owners, I recommend that, for a trial period, the pub is only permitted to serve alcoholic beverages from 11am until 1pm, and from 5pm till 7pm. This will reduce the risk of problems developing. Providing there are no problems with anti-social behaviour, littering or rowdiness, then we could look to review the opening hours with a view to extending them.

Below I have provided you with some final hints and tips on how to create an effective report, along with a number of sample exercises to help get you more familiar with the process.

I firmly believe that this course of action is in the best interests of the centre, its staff and the customers. I am prepared to take full responsibility for monitoring the situation once the pub has been opened. I will keep you updated on my progress.

Important tips to help you structure a good report

• Remember that you are being assessed against your ability to communicate effectively in writing. This means creating a report that is concise, relevant, easy to read and free from errors;

• Make sure you answer the question;

• Aim to make zero grammar, spelling or punctuation errors. If you are unsure about a word, do not use it;

• Create your report using a beginning, middle and an end as I have suggested;

• The amount that you write is down to you. Your focus should be on the quality of the report rather than quantity.

Now that you know how to create a written report, try the sample exercises on the following pages. I have provided you

with a template following each exercise to help you create your report.

Sample Report Writing Exercise 2

You are the security deputy for a fictitious retail park. You have been asked to compile a report for your superior officer, in relation to a number of complaints that have been made by customers at the centre. The complaints are in regards to a number of difficult teenagers, who are terrorising shoppers. In the last 6 months, visiting numbers are down by over 35%. Shop owners are also complaining, because their profits have been reduced as a result of this problem.

CCTV evidence shows that the gang of teenagers have been hanging around smoking on the shopping park corners, making insulting comments towards shoppers and harassing them for spare change. In order to try and resolve the situation, the county newspaper wants to create a report on the incidents, and what the centre's security plan to do about them. In order to write this, they have arranged an interview with your manager.

Your report should detail your main findings and also your recommendations as to how the situation can be resolved. Use the template on the next page to construct your response.

Written report sample exercise 3

You are the police liaison officer for a fictitious retail centre. The manager of the centre has received several requests from customers, who are complaining about a number of different issues. First, there are a number of complaints from customers who claim that local children have been seen on the premises during school hours. They believe these children to be truanting from school, and want to involve the Anti-Truancy group in attempts to fix this. Secondly, in response to other complaints, the local police force have claimed that anti-social behavioural incidents at the centre have risen by 20% in the last 6 weeks alone. CCTV cameras have confirmed these reports.

You are to create a report for your manager that details your main findings and your recommendations. Use the template on the next page to create your response.

<u>Written report sample exercise 4</u>

You are the health and safety officer for a fictitious retail centre. A recent incident at the centre led to an inspection from the Fire Service, who discovered that a large number of the fire escapes at the centre had been blocked off by cardboard and other waste, which had been placed there by shop owners. Furthermore, they reported that the centre housekeeping was far below the acceptable standard, and presented a serious health and safety risk. While the obstructions were removed, and the Fire Service will not be taking any further action, your manager is concerned that this type of incident will happen again.

He has asked you to create a report detailing your recommendations as to how this type of incident can be prevented in the future, and also how the standard of housekeeping can be improved. Use the template on the next page to create your response.

Case Study Analysis

The second exercise that you might need to take at the GCHQ assessment centre is a case study analysis. A case study analysis is similar to the previous report writing exercise, but will require greater attention to detail and logical thinking. The case study analysis will also be intelligence based, meaning that you'll be asked to provide recommendations on a fictional major crime or terrorism related incident, and not simply a case of anti-social behaviour.

Due to the nature of the exercise, you can expect the case study analysis to be lengthier than that of the report writing. GCHQ do not expect you to be a high level expert in dealing with criminals and terrorists, so they will provide you with enough information to help you come to critical decisions. However, they will also provide you with enough information to steer you off track. Your job is essentially to sift through the information, and establish what is relevant and what is not, before providing logical solutions to the problems presented.

One of the best ways to go about dealing with a case study exercise, is to highlight all of the key points. Remember that you will be given a lot of irrelevant information. You need to highlight the key points so that you can come to quick and logical solutions for dealing with them.

Below we have listed an example case study. As you go through the case study, highlight the points which you think need to be dealt with as a matter of importance.

Sample Case Study Analysis: Exercise 1

You are a senior intelligence analyst at GCHQ. For the past year, you have been working on a case involving a Croydon based drug smuggling gang. Recent events have seen a breakthrough in the case.

The gang first came to GCHQ's attention in late summer of 2014. After intercepting and decoding mailed messages between a known supplier and a member of the gang (who were unknown to GCHQ at the time), a surveillance operation was launched by MI5 and an agent, named Marcus Smith, was posted to infiltrate the gang. Marcus had brown hair, and was fairly experienced in operations such as this. He lived with his wife and children at 72 Grove Close, Hackney.

After a few months, GCHQ obtained circumstantial evidence of what was believed to be a large scale drug operation taking place. Unfortunately, it appears that the gang were tipped off, and an attempt to raid their shared flat brought up no results. The flat was unfurnished, and there was thick mould on the walls. The agent posted with the group has also gone missing. The investigation has been criticised by certain members of GCHQ, who believe that the organisation are wasting time and resources on such a smaller target. GCHQ are also involved in monitoring a number of other threats across the country, and have stopped several this year alone.

Further investigation from GCHQ and MI5 has revealed potential backlinks between the Croydon gang and a number of other wanted criminals across the city of London, all related to drugs. As the investigation has progressed, it has become apparent that 'the Croydon Crew' are simply a smaller pawn in a much larger operation. MI5 believe that they have the

leaders of this operation in their sights, and have posted another agent to infiltrate the group. Meanwhile, GCHQ have continued to monitor the operations of the Croydon Crew.

A recent breakthrough in the last week has seen a member of the GCHQ team gain access to the email history of a high level member of the gang, revealing a substantial list of drug purchases that goes all the way back to 2010. The drug purchases are for class C drugs only. The emails are believed to be enough to arrest the entire Croydon Crew. There were also emails from the individual to his relatives, promising to meet them at the weekend, and online receipts for purchased clothing. MI5 believe that it would be better to wait before making any arrests. They fear for the life of their agent, and believe that arresting the Croydon Crew would damage the chances of stopping a higher level target. The local police force are also frustrated. They believe they themselves have evidence, and are awaiting a decision from intelligence services as to whether they should move in. They have given them a deadline of a week before they do so.

Your manager, Mr Smith, has asked you to file a report on what you believe is the best solution.

How to answer this

When answering a case study analysis, the first thing you need to do is separate the irrelevant facts from the relevant facts.

Let's take a look at the passage, and rule out the **irrelevant information,** from that which could influence our decision.

Irrelevant information

'Marcus had brown hair, and was fairly experienced in operations such as this. He lived with his wife and children at 72 Grove Close, Hackney.'

'The flat was unfurnished, and there was thick mould on the walls.'

'GCHQ are also involved in monitoring a number of other threats across the country, and have stopped several this year alone.'

'There were also emails from the individual to his relatives, promising to meet them at the weekend, and online receipts for purchased clothing.'

We don't need to know any of the above, because none of it has any bearing on our decision. Take a pen and cross out the above extracts from the text. Now, let's look at the most important bits of information, which do have an impact on our decision.

Important Information

'The agent posted with the group has also gone missing.'

This is important because it indicates that the failure of the previous investigation may have led to a loss of life.

'GCHQ obtained circumstantial evidence of what was believed to be a large scale drug operation taking place.'

This is important because it indicates that GCHQ only had circumstantial evidence to go by, and not anything concrete. The rest of the passage does not indicate that GCHQ have any solid evidence for anything other than class C drugs.

'It has become apparent that 'the Croydon Crew' are simply a smaller pawn in a much larger operation.'

This is important because it indicates that the special services could be onto a much larger drug bust than initially anticipated.

'The drug purchases are for class C drugs only.'

This is important because it indicates that the gang will not receive a significant penalty for these purchases.

'They fear for the life of their agent, and believe that arresting the Croydon Crew would damage the chances of stopping a higher level target.'

This is important because it indicates that the life of another person could be at risk if the arrest is carried out. It could also ruin the chances of arresting a more dangerous threat.

Finally, let's take a look at other pieces of evidence which could also be taken into account when reaching a decision on this case.

Other evidence

'For the past year, you have been working on a case involving a Croydon based drug smuggling gang.'

The fact that GCHQ have invested over a year's worth of work into the case could be considered as important.

'The investigation has been criticised by certain members of GCHQ, who believe that the organisation are wasting time and resources on such a smaller target.'

The fact that some members of GCHQ are unhappy about the amount of time spent on what they believe to be a minor operation could be considered as important. GCHQ is a team.

'The local police force are also frustrated, and are awaiting a decision from intelligence services as to whether they should move in.'

The fact that the police force are frustrated by the amount of indecision or lack of progress could be considered as important. GCHQ and MI5 need to maintain a good relationship with local law enforcement.

Pros and Cons

Another way of planning for this type of question is to separate the evidence into a pros and cons list. On the following page, we have created a table that weighs up the pros and cons of the situation.

Should the police force make the arrest?

<u>**Pros**</u>	<u>**Cons**</u>
GCHQ have been working on the case for over a year.	One agent has already gone missing as a result of the failure of the previous investigation. Another agent is at risk.
The local police believe they have enough evidence to arrest the gang.	
If an arrest is not authorised, the local police force will become even more impatient.	GCHQ only had circumstantial evidence to back up their investigation before, and only have minor evidence of criminal activity from this one.
Arresting the gang could lead to further arrests much higher up in the chain.	Arresting the Croydon Gang could lead to other, more dangerous drug smugglers getting away.

Constructing Your Report

Now that you've planned your answer, it's time to construct your report. It's important to remember that, technically, there are no right or wrong answers here. Many of the scenarios that you encounter in the case analysis exercises are scenarios where the decision could swing either way, you simply need to provide a logical proposal that outlines the reasons that you have made your decision.

GCHQ don't expect you to make critical intelligence decisions right off the bat, but they do expect you to think in an analytical and logical manner, using sensible reasoning to back up your decisions. This is where the pros and cons table will be extremely useful. A table such as this allows you to see all of the evidence that you will use to support your argument, which in turn will help you construct a solid and logical response to the question.

Take a look at our sample response to this exercise below.

Sample Response

Dear Mr Smith,

I have looked through the evidence from the Croydon Crew drug smuggling case, and have come to the decision that I believe it would not be in the best interests of GCHQ to authorise an arrest. The reasons that I believe this are as follows:

Firstly, I do not believe that GCHQ has collected enough evidence to support their arrest warrant. While it is true that class C drugs are a criminal offence, and possession can result in up to 2 years in prison, GCHQ entered this case on the basis that it was leading to something more substantial. There is potential for this to happen, but in order for this to come about, the arrest needs to be put off for the time being.

Secondly, with the prior point in mind, it is important to consider the implications that an arrest could have. MI5 have rightly pointed out that the last time the intelligence services moved too fast, one of their agents went missing, and they still have another agent posted in the field. It's likely that this alerted the gang to the fact that they were under investigation, and damaged the operation as a whole.

Thirdly, if there is a chance to make an arrest on a higher level target, then I believe it would be wise to wait for the opportunity to do so, and not damage the chances of this by moving too early. As of yet, we simply don't have enough evidence.

When making this decision, I have taken all factors into account. This includes the fact that the local police force are growing impatient to make an arrest, and that GCHQ have been working on this case for over a year. The latter, I believe, only means that we should exercise more caution and make sure we have substantial evidence to support our claims.

On a final note, I have been made aware that there are several members of GCHQ who are struggling to understand the importance of this operation. While this shouldn't have a bearing on our decision, GCHQ is a team, and therefore it's important that these individuals are briefed fully and helped to understand why we are investigating the Croydon Crew.

Now that you've seen how to go about answering a question like this, let's have a look at another similar excise.

Sample Case Study Analysis: Exercise 2

You are a senior intelligence analyst at GCHQ. A month ago, hackers broke into the database of Northern Star Banks, one of the biggest banks in the world. They stole the data of thousands of Northern Star customers, and in the days following, used this to take money from customer accounts that amounted to over £600,000. Northern Star have promised that all customers will be refunded in full, and have asked the UK intelligence services to find out who was responsible. There are 4 main suspects for the hacking:

Suspect 1: OAH Group. Only Anoynomous Hackers (OAH) are a well-known hacking group with a history of pulling off 'statement hacks'. In the past, their targets have included smaller local branches and even some bigger banks. However, they have never stolen any funds or customer data. Usually, OAH simply hack into company websites and leave a message that reads 'OAH Property'. The motivation behind OAH hacks is believed to be for infamy. That is to say, OAH wants to put their name out there. Since news about the hacking broke, OAH have released a statement denying any culpability. The question is, can you trust them?

Suspect 2: GNOB. GNOB are a right wing, animal rights group. While not technically a criminal organisation, they are highly radical and have been known to hack targets in the past. In the week before the attack, the chairman of Northern Star was accosted by members of GNOB on his way to work, for wearing a beaver fur overcoat. Northern Star are also the official sponsors of various hunting gear specialists, and their logo can be seen on equipment such as guns, tracking overalls and boots. This has brought the bank a great deal of

controversy. GNOB have made no official statements since the attack. On their official website, GNOB lists their political aims as:

- *The destruction of wealth, in order to bring world peace.*

- *The breaking of the European Union.*

- *The extermination of hunters and those who are cruel to animals.*

Some officials within GCHQ believe that GNOB could be holding the customer's money to ransom, to try and force Northern Star away from sponsoring hunting activities. Could this be the reason for the attack?

Suspect 3: Mardan Mob. *The Mardan Mob are a Staffordshire based criminal gang, who have been under suspicion from GCHQ for quite some time. While GCHQ do not yet have solid evidence to prove their suspicions correct, it is believed that in the last 2 years, the crimes of the Mardan Mob have escalated in seriousness. While they began by robbing houses and then selling on stolen possessions, in recent months GCHQ believes them to be behind a spate of jewel heists in the Staffordshire area. GCHQ also has reason to believe that the Mardan Mob have moved into arms dealing, and could now be purchasing weapons from suspect terrorists abroad. Intelligence intercepted communications between a member of the mob and a suspected terrorist, indicating that an arms deal was due to take place within the next 2 weeks.*

Last year, the leader of the mob – Derek Banning, was arrested on drug trafficking charges. By request from the

intelligence services, Northern Star locked his account with them, and have since refused numerous attempts from other members of the gang to get back in. With their assets frozen, and a high value arms deal just around the corner, could the Mob be responsible for the hacking?

Suspect 4: Samantha Manning. *Samantha Manning was a long term employee at Northern Star. Northern Star themselves have brought her to GCHQ's attention, as they believe there is a chance that she could be responsible for the hacking. Mrs Manning was fired 2 days after the theft took place, in the wake of an internal investigation from Northern Star. Northern Star claim that Mrs Manning has a history of risk taking behaviour, and while this has never been an issue so far, their investigation indicates that Mrs Manning has been extremely reckless in the past few months. The reason they believe this is as follows:*

- *Mrs Manning has been leaving critical deadlines until the last minute, leaving herself less than a few days to complete them.*

- *Mrs Manning has been spending several nights a week at her local casino, and as a result took a cash withdrawal from the online digital safe for £7000 just 3 days before the attack. She did this without the bank's permission, which amounts to stealing. Northern Star are filing criminal charges against her.*

- *Mrs Manning had been using her work computer to look for ways to accumulate large amounts of wealth, in a very short amount of time.*

The head of intelligence, Mr Smith, wants you to look closely

at these suspects. He has asked you to produce a report outlining who should be investigated as a matter of priority, in which order, and why.

How To Plan Your Answer

This is a priority based case analysis question, which simply means that you need to put the different suspects in order of importance. In this case, you need to arrange them according to how likely you believe they are to have committed the crime, and explain your reasons why. The best way to do this is to arrange the suspects into your own list, with bullets points indicating why you think each one could be responsible.

For example:

1. Mardan Mob

Motivations: Have a history of serious criminal incidents, might want revenge against Northern Star, and are known to be short on cash. Have an integral criminal operation running in 2 weeks' time, which will require significant funds.

Evidence against: No evidence to suggest they have moved into hacking.

2. GNOB

Motivations: Want revenge against Northern Star for breaching animal rights/hunting, have openly threatened the chairman of Northern Star in the past, highly radical, have a history of hacking attacks in the past, may be holding the customers money to ransom until Northern Star abstain from funding hunters.

Evidence against: Claim to want the destruction of wealth/ abhor money, so why would they steal it? If it's been a month since the attack, holding the money to ransom does not make sense without a statement to back it up.

3. Samantha Manning

Motivations: Shown to be a risk taker, has been behaving recklessly in the past few months, already stole £7000 from Northern Star, worked at the bank meaning that she had easier access to customer accounts/database, was using work computer for self-financing research.

Evidence against: Already stole £7000 in the week leading up to the attack, £600,000 more is quite a leap.

4. OAH.

Motivations: Have committed several high profile hacks in the past, have shown they will go to criminal lengths to further their reputation.

Evidence against: Crime doesn't fit the profile of a normal OAH attack, OAH have released a statement specifically denying involvement – where ordinarily this would be something they'd want to take credit for, in order to put their name out there.

Now, using the above list, take a look at our sample response to this question.

Sample Response

Dear Mr Smith,

I have reviewed the case file on the Northern Star hacking case, and attach my suggestions below.

My first priority of investigation in this case would be the Mardan Mob. The reasons that I believe the Mob should be our top priority are as follows. The Mob are well known to GCHQ and believed to be behind a string of extremely serious criminal incidents. These incidents have risen in the past few months, and have extended to jewellery heists and arms dealing. Evidence suggests that the Mob have arranged a high profile arms deal within the next 2 weeks, and therefore it goes without saying that they will need funds for this to take place. By robbing Northern Star, who previously froze their assets in the first place, the Mob can a) take revenge on an organisation they feel has wronged them, and b) secure the funds they need. While there is no evidence to suggest that the Mob have ever engaged in hacking previously, I believe they are the most likely suspect in this case.

My second priority in this investigation would be GNOB. The main reason that I believe this is because GNOB have a) a genuine motivation to try and harm Northern Star, and b) have already threatened and harassed the chairman of Northern Star in the past. Alongside this, GNOB have a history of hacking attacks, and are known to be highly radical.

For these reasons, I believe we have strong cause to suspect them. Despite this, there is also some evidence to suggest that GNOB might not be responsible. Contrary to some people's belief, it is my view that if GNOB were holding Northern Star to ransom, they would have released a statement by now. It has been over a month since the hacking took place. Furthermore, stealing or accumulating money does not fit with GNOB's political agenda.

My third priority would be Samantha Manning. The reason that she is my third priority is that while her reckless behaviour needs to be considered, the fact of the matter is that she had already stolen money 2 days before the incident took place. We know that Mrs Manning had amassed gambling debts, and was behaving recklessly, but it is quite a leap to go from stealing £7000, to stealing £600,000 2 days later. Having said this, Mrs Manning's behaviour warrants suspicion and she is already under criminal investigation. She had behaved recklessly, and had easier access to the stolen money. Therefore, she ranks above OAH as a suspect,

My final suspect, and lowest priority, would be OAH. I believe that there are more reasons not to suspect OAH than to believe they are guilty of the crime. Firstly, the crime does not fit with OAH's modus operandi. As we know, OAH's typical behaviour is to hack a company's website and put their name up on the front page. By doing this, they believe they will gain notoriety. OAH have also taken the unusual step of denying their involvement in the crime. Given their motivations for hacking in the first place, I believe this is indicative of the fact that they aren't guilty.

When answering case analysis questions, always remember that it's not whether you are right or wrong that counts. What matters is that you can support your answers with logical and sensible reasoning.

Numerical Reasoning

The next exercise that you will have to take is a Numerical Reasoning test. In chapter 4, we provided you with a brief introduction to Numerical Reasoning. To help you out, let's recap:

A Numerical Reasoning test is designed to assess mathematical knowledge through number-related assessments. These assessments can be of different difficulty levels, and will all vary depending at which stage of the process you are taking the test. Once you reach the assessment centre stage of the process, you can expect to take harder Numerical Reasoning questions.

Numerical Reasoning tests cover a wide range of mathematical formulae, so it is imperative that you have practiced as much as you can before attending the assessment centre. In order to pass a Numerical Reasoning test, you will need to be proficient in areas such as:

- Adding and subtracting.

- Fractions, percentages and decimals.

- Areas and perimeters.

- Data analysis.

- Mean, Mode, Median and Range.

- Ratio and time.

- Number sequences

- Multiplication and long multiplication.

- Division and long division.

- Mass, density and volume.

Have a go at our sample Numerical Reasoning questions. Once you've completed the test, check how many you've got right using the answer sheet provided.

Question 1

The diagram below shows the plan of a building site. All angles are right angles.

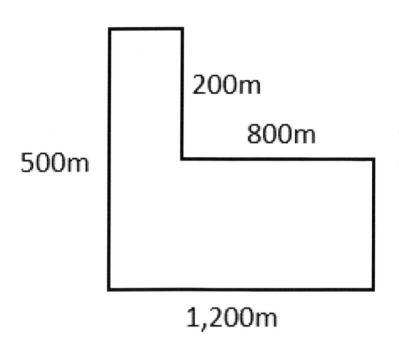

What is the area of the building site?
Give your answer in hectares.

1 hectare = 10,000m² = 2.47 acres.

A	B	C	D
60 hectares	40 hectares	44 hectares	4.4 hectares

Question 2

Look carefully for the pattern, and then choose which pair of numbers comes next.

1,   3,   6,   10,   15,   21,   28

A	B	C	D
42, 56	42, 48	30, 36	36, 45

Question 3

Government spending on "Education services" and "Health services" was 56.3 billion pounds and 106.7 billion respectively for the year 2009-2010. In the same year, the Government spending on "Debt Interests" was 22.22% of the spending on "Education services", and the spending on "Education services", "Health services" and "Debt Interests" constituted 50% of the total spending by the Government.

What was the Government's approximate total spending for the year 2009-2010?

A	B	C	D
551 billion pounds	615 billion pounds	351 billion pounds	435 billion pounds

Question 4

The Siberian tiger population in Country A is 60% of the Siberian tiger population in Country B. The population of Siberian tigers in Country C is 50% of that in the Country A.

If the Siberian tiger population in Country C is 420, what is the Siberian tiger population in Country B?

A	B	C	D
1,400	1,200	1,000	1,600

Question 5

If the dollar amount of sales at Store W was $456,250 for 2011, what was the dollar amount of sales at that store for 2013?

Annual Percent Change in Dollar Amount of Sales at Five Fashion Stores From 2011 to 2013		
Store	**Percent Change From 2011 to 2012**	**Percent Change From 2012 to 2013**
U	18	-10
V	17	-7
W	16	6
X	20	-5
Y	-15	-8

Answer [   ]

Question 6

Below is a table representing the income of industries in billions of pounds over a five year period.

	Year 1	Year 2	Year 3	Year 4	Year 5
Financing	65	82	93	100	112
Telecommunications	18	21	27	34	38
Engineering	37	58	60	64	68
Agriculture	26	26	30	30	55
Media	59	60	72	78	75
Manufacturing	33	38	41	30	27
Transportation	48	48	49	56	60

Which industry had the largest increase in amount of income between Year 2 and Year 3?

A	B	C	D	E
Financing	Transportation	Media	Agriculture	Engineering

Question 7

Below is a table of the total staff at Company A (Staff Distribution).

	HR	Sales	Finance	Media	Distribution	TOTAL(%)
Year 1	21	8	19	32	20	100
Year 2	28	11	17	28	16	100
Year 3	16	21	19	26	18	100
Year 4	14	29	21	14	22	100
Year 5	4	9	25	38	24	100
Year 6	20	27	25	12	16	100

In Year 4, there were 406 people employed in Finance. How many people in total were employed in Year 4 in the department of Sales? Rounded to a whole person.

Answer

Question 8

In July, Ryan worked a total of 40 hours, in August he worked 46.5 hours – by what percentage did Ryan's working hours increase in August?

A	B	C	D
16.25%	165%	1.625%	25%

Question 9

What is one quarter of 6 hours?

A	B	C	D
1 hour and 30 minutes	95 minutes	180 minutes	1 hour and 20 minutes

Question 10

The following table shows the prices of a travel agents holiday prices for booking holidays for next year.

HOLIDAY PRICES				
Types of Holiday Deals	Turkey	Mexico	America	Spain
All inclusive	£276pp	£720pp	£880pp	£320pp
Half board	£220pp	£640pp	£795pp	£275pp
Self-Catering	£180pp	£550pp	£620pp	£235pp

How much more would it cost if three all-inclusive holidays each for two people to Mexico were booked, as opposed to one booking for a self-catering holiday to Turkey for five people?

A	B	C	D
£1,250	£3,420	£9,000	£4,500

Answers to Numerical Reasoning

Q1. C = 44 hectares

EXPLANATION = Work out the area of the whole shape: 1200 x 500 = 600,000

Work out the area of the missing rectangle (to make a complete rectangle): 800 x 200 = 160,000

So, 600,000 − 160,000 = 440,000m².

440,000m² in hectares = 440,000 ÷ 10,000 = 44 hectares.

Q2. D = 36 and 45

EXPLANATION = this is a triangular number sequence. It uses the pattern of the number of dots which forms a triangle. By adding another row of dots (which increases by 1 each time) and counting all the dots, we can find the next number of the sequence.

Q3. C = 351 billion pounds

EXPLANATION = Education services = 56.3 billion pounds and Health services = 106.7 billion pounds.

22.22% of 56.3 = 56.3 ÷ 100 x 22.22 = 12.50986 (Round up = 12.51).

The total of Education, Health and Debt Interests = 175.51 billion pounds.

The total Government spending = 175.51 x 100 ÷ 50 = 351.02.

So, the approximate total = 351 billion pounds.

Q4. A = 1,400

EXPLANATION = Siberian tiger population in Country C is 50% of that in Country A.

If country C is 420, Country A = 420 x 100 ÷ 50 = 840.

So, if Country A = 840 and is 60% of the population in Country B, Country B = 840 x 100 ÷ 60 = 1,400.

Q5. $561,005

EXPLANATION = for Store W, in 2011 = $456,250. In order to get from 2011 to 2012, we see a 16% increase. So, 456,250 ÷ 100 x 116(%) = 529,250.

To get from 2012 to 2013, we see a 6% increase. So, 529,250 ÷ 100 x 106 = 561,005.

So, the store amount of sales for Store W in 2013 is $561,005.

Q6. C = Media

EXPLANATION = you need to work out the difference for each industry from Year 2 to Year 3.

Financing = increase = 11

Telecommunications = increase = 6

Engineering = increase = 2

Agriculture = increase = 4

Media = increase = 12

Manufacturing = increase = 3

Transportation = increase = 1

So, the largest increase between Year 2 and Year 3 was in the industry of Media.

Q7. 560

EXPLANATION = in order to work out the number of people working in Sales in Year 4, you need to work out the total number of employees in that year.

So, 406 (number of people employed in Finance) x 100 ÷ 21 (percentage of Finance) = 1933.333. To the nearest whole person = 1933.

So, 1933 ÷ 100 x 29 (number of employees in Sales) = 560.57. To the nearest whole person = 560.

Q8. A = 16.25%

EXPLANATION = To tackle this problem first we calculate the difference in hours between the new and old numbers. 46.5 - 40 hours = 6.5 hours. We can see that Ryan worked 6.5 hours more in August than he did in July – this is his increase.

To work out the increase as a percentage it is now necessary to divide the increase by the original (January) number: 6.5 ÷ 40 = 0.1625

Finally, to get the percentage we multiply the answer by 100. This simply means moving the decimal place two columns to the right.

0.1625 × 100 = 16.25.

Ryan therefore worked 16.25% more hours in August than he did in July.

Q9. A = 90 minutes

EXPLANATION = 6 (hours) x (60 (minutes) = 360 minutes. So, 360 (minutes) ÷ 4 (1/4) = 90 minutes.

Q10. B = £3,420

EXPLANATION = Self-catering holiday to Turkey for 5 people = 180 x 5 = 900.

All-inclusive holiday to Mexico for 2 people = 720 x 2 = 1440. Booked three times = 1440 x 3 = 4320.

So, 4320 – 900 = 3,420.

Verbal Reasoning

The next exercise that you will have to take is a Verbal Reasoning test. In chapter 4, we provided you with a brief introduction to Verbal Reasoning. To help you out, let's recap:

A Verbal Reasoning test will assess how well you can ascertain key information, from large passages of text. The questions will require you to draw logical or inarguable conclusions from the passage. Since you have now reached the assessment centre stage, you can expect the type of Verbal Reasoning questions to be harder, and also to follow a slightly different format. The new questions that you will need to answer are relatively straightforward, and still require the same skillset; however you will need to concentrate fully in order to succeed.

Before we begin, let's take a look at a sample question.

Sample Verbal Reasoning Question

Read the following text before answering the questions as either TRUE, FALSE or CANNOT SAY from the information given.

Passage - Basic holiday rights for employees

There is a minimum right to paid holiday, but your employer may offer more than this. All employees are entitled to a minimum of 5.6 weeks paid leave per year. Those employees who work for five days a week are entitled to 28 days per year annual leave (capped at a statutory maximum of 28 days for all working patterns). Employees who work part-time are entitled to the same level of holiday pro rata (5.6 times your normal working week) e.g. 16.8 days for someone working three days a week.

All employees will start building up holiday entitlement as soon as they start work with the employer. The employer has the right to control when you take your holiday but you must get paid the same level of pay whilst on holiday. When you finish working for an employer you get paid for any holiday you have not taken. The employer may include bank and public holidays in your minimum entitlement. You continue to be entitled to your holiday leave throughout any additional maternity/paternity leave and adoption leave.

Q1. An employer may not offer you more than the minimum paid holiday. True, false or impossible to say?

Q2. In addition to paternity leave you are entitled to your normal holiday. True, false or impossible to say?

Q3. All employees only start building up holiday leave 5.6 weeks after commencement of employment. True, false or impossible to say?

Q4. Employees who receive more than the minimum holiday entitlement are often grateful to their employer. True, false or impossible to say?

How To Answer These Questions

The important thing to remember is that you should base your answers **only** on the passage of text provided. Let's break each question down individually:

Q1. An employer may not offer you more than the minimum paid holiday.

By reading the passage carefully you will note that the following sentence is demonstrated in the first paragraph.

"There is a minimum right to paid holiday, but your employer may offer more than this."

We can deduce from the passage that Question 1 is in fact FALSE, simply because an employer may offer more than the minimum paid holiday. Fortunately for us the first question related to the very first sentence in the passage. However, in the majority of cases this will not be the norm.

Q2. In addition to paternity leave you are entitled to your normal holiday.

By reading the passage carefully you will note that the following sentence relates to the last paragraph.

"You continue to be entitled to your holiday leave throughout any additional maternity/paternity leave and adoption leave."

We can deduce from the passage that Question 2 is in fact TRUE. An employee is entitled to their holiday leave throughout paternity leave. Question 2 is a very good example of how 'scanning' the passage can save you time. You will note that the word 'paternity' is only used once throughout the entire passage. By scanning the passage quickly in search of specific keywords or phrases you will be able to reach the section of the passage that relates to the question and thus answer the question far quicker than reading the entire passage.

Q3. All employees only start building up holiday leave 5.6 weeks after commencement of employment.

By reading the passage carefully you will note that the following sentence relates to the first paragraph.

"All employees will start building up holiday as soon as they start work with the employer."

We can deduce from the passage that Question 3 is in fact FALSE based on the information provided. An employee starts building up holiday as soon as they start work with the employer, not 5.6 weeks after commencement of employment.

Q4. Employees who receive more than the minimum holiday entitlement are often grateful to their employer.

By reading the passage carefully you will note that none of the content relates to the question. At no point does it state that employees who receive more than the minimum holiday

entitlement are often grateful to their employer, or otherwise. Therefore, the answer is CANNOT SAY based on the information provided.

Although it is probably true in real life that most employees would be grateful for receiving more than the minimum holiday requirement, we can only answer the question based solely on the information provided in the passage.

Now, have a go our sample test below. Make sure to compare your answers with the answer sheet following the test.

Verbal Reasoning Sample Test

*Read the following passages before answering the questions as either **TRUE**, **FALSE** or **CANNOT SAY** from the information given.*

Analysts prove forecasters wrong

The Office for National Statistics said internet shopping and sales of household goods had been better in October compared with previous months. However, sales of clothing and footwear, where many retailers cut prices before Christmas, were particularly weak.

The increase came as a surprise to many analysts who were predicting a 0.4% fall in internet shopping and sales of household goods. The rise meant that retail sales volumes in the three months to January were up by 2.6% on the previous quarter. The final quarter of the year is a better guide to the underlying trend than one month's figures.

Some analysts cautioned that the heavy seasonal adjustment of the raw spending figures at the turn of the year made interpreting the data difficult. Even so, the government will be relieved that spending appears to be holding up despite the squeeze on incomes caused by high inflation, rising unemployment, a weak housing market and the crisis in the eurozone.

Retail sales account for less than half of total consumer spending and do not include the purchase of cars or eating out. The ONS said that its measure of inflation in the high street – the annual retail sales deflator – fell to 2.2% last month, its lowest level since November 2009. Ministers are hoping that lower inflation will boost real income growth during the course of 2012.

A - True	B - False	C - Cannot Say
Circle A if the question is TRUE from the information provided.	Circle B if the question is FALSE from the information provided.	Circle C if CANNOT SAY from the information provided.

Question 1. Ministers hope that higher inflation will boost real income growth during 2012.

A	B	C

Question 2. Analyst's predicted a 0.4% rise in the sales of household goods.

A	B	C

Question 3. The crisis in the eurozone is contributing to the squeeze on incomes.

A	B	C

Long-service payments

Employees who attain fifteen years' continuous service between 7th November 2003 and 30th June 2007 shall qualify for the long-service payment at the rate applicable at the time. Employees who are promoted to a higher role during this period will cease to qualify for the payment but will receive a minimum pay increase on promotion of £300 per annum, which will be achieved through partial protection of the long-service payment.

Where the pay assimilation process on 7th November 2003 created a basic pay increase of more than 7%, and the employee was in receipt of the long-service payment, the payment has been reduced with effect from that date by the amount that the increase exceeded 7%. The consequent pay rates were set out in circular NJC/01/04.

Pay protection for employees on the retained duty system

Where an employee on the retained duty system has not received a pay increase of at least 7% (for the same pattern and level of activity) following full implementation of the pay award effective from 7th November 2003, the fire and rescue authority may introduce arrangements to ensure that such an increase is achieved.

Acting up and temporary promotion

The NJC recognises that in the early stages of implementing the Integrated Personal Development System it may, on occasions, be difficult to apply the principles at Paragraph 19 of Section 4 Part B. Fire and rescue authorities, employees and trade unions should therefore adopt a co-operative and common sense approach to any problems that might arise.

Question 4. If an employee who is on the retained duty system has not received a pay increase of at least 7% following the introduction of the pay award, the fire and rescue service must introduce arrangements to ensure that such an increase is achieved.

A	B	C

Question 5. Employees who attain fifteen years' continuous service between 7th November 2003 and 30th June 2008 shall qualify for the long-service payment at the rate applicable at the time.

A	B	C

Question 6. The pay assimilation process on 7th November 2003 created a basic pay increase for all employees of more than 7%.

A	B	C

Data warehouses

A data warehouse is the main source of information for an organisation's historical data. Its historical data is often referred to as its corporate memory. As an example of how a data warehouse can be put to good use, an organisation would use the information stored in its data warehouse to find out how many particular stock items they sold on a particular day in a particular year. They could also ascertain which employees were off sick on any given day or any given year. The data stored within the warehouse contains essential information so that managers can make appropriate management decisions.

A data warehouse is normally large in size as the information stored usually focuses on basic, structured and organised data. Some of the characteristics of the data in a data warehouse are as follows:

Time-variant - changes to the data in the database are tracked and recorded so that reports can be produced showing changes over time;

Non-volatile - the data in the database is never over-written or deleted but is retained for future reporting;

Integrated - the database contains data from most or all of an organisation's operational applications and this data is useful and meaningful for further processing and analysis.

Question 7. Integrated and non-volatile data form some of the characteristics of a data warehouse.

A	B	C

Question 8. It is not possible to identify which employees were on sick leave from the information stored in a data warehouse.

A	B	C

Question 9. Corporate memory is an alternative name given to historical data.

A	B	C

The importance of health and safety in the workplace

You must protect the safety and health of everyone in your workplace, including people with disabilities, and provide welfare facilities for your employees.

Basic things you need to consider are outlined below.

Welfare facilities

For your employees' well-being you need to provide:

- toilets and hand basins, with soap and towels or a hand-dryer;

- drinking water;

- a place to store clothing (and somewhere to change if special clothing is worn for work);

- somewhere to rest and eat meals.

Health issues

To have a healthy working environment, make sure there is:

- good ventilation – a supply of fresh, clean air drawn from outside or a ventilation system;

- a reasonable working temperature (usually at least 16°C, or 13°C for strenuous work, unless other laws require lower temperatures);

- lighting suitable for the work being carried out;

- enough room space and suitable workstations and seating;

- a clean workplace with appropriate waste containers.

Safety issues

To keep your workplace safe you must:

- properly maintain your premises and work equipment;

- keep floors and traffic routes free from obstruction;

- have windows that can be opened and also cleaned safely;

- make sure that any transparent (eg glass) doors or walls are protected or made of safety material.

Question 10. It is the responsibility of the employee for keeping a workplace safe.

A	B	C

Question 11. Providing the employee with a suitable workstation is a consideration for the employer when making the workplace safe.

A	B	C

Question 12. An employer must ensure that all floor surfaces are non-slip in order to prevent slips, trips and falls.

A	B	C

Magistrate training

The entire selection process for becoming a magistrate can take approximately 12 months, sometimes longer depending on the area.

Once you have been accepted you will be required to undertake a comprehensive training course which is usually held over a 3-day period (18 hours). During this course you will learn the necessary skills that are required in order to become a magistrate.

The training is normally carried out by the Justice Clerk who is responsible for the court. He/she will usually be the legal advisor during your magistrate sittings. They will help you to develop all the necessary skills required in order to carry out your duties professionally and competently.

You will carry out your training as part of a group with other people who have been recruited at the same time as you. This is extremely beneficial as it will allow you to learn in a safe environment.

Training will be given using a variety of methods, which may include pre-course reading, small-group work, use of case studies, computer-based training and CCTV. It is recognised that magistrates are volunteers and that their time is valuable, so every effort is made to provide all training at times and places convenient to trainees. The Ministry of Justice booklet 'Serving as a Magistrate' has more information about the magistracy and the role of magistrates.

Question 13. The comprehensive training course for becoming a magistrate usually consists of 3 days which is divided into 6 hours training per day.

A	B	C

Question 14. An applicant can find out more about the role of a magistrate by reading the Ministry of Justice booklet 'Serving as a Magistrate'.

A	B	C

Question 15. The selection process for becoming a magistrate will take no longer than 12 months.

A	B	C

How to enrol in our online sellers' programme

To enrol in our online sellers' programme, you must have an email account, access to the Internet, have a UK distribution facility and also hold the full UK distribution rights to the item(s) you want to sell.

You must have a UK bank account capable of receiving payments via electronic bank transfer (BACS), as this is the only method of payment we offer. Each product you wish to sell in our programme must meet our minimum eligibility standards. These standards relate to quality, value, subject matter, production standards and compliance with intellectual property laws. We reserve the right to remove any products if they do not meet our standards. You are not permitted to sell any products that are deemed to be pornographic or racist.

Any books that you wish to sell via our sellers' programme must have a 10 or 13 digit ISBN number and applicable barcode printed on the back of the book in the bottom right-hand corner.

The barcode must scan to match the ISBN of the book. If the item you want to sell is a music CD then the CD must be in a protective case which meets the relevant British Standard.

The title and artist name must be printed on and readable from the spine (the thin side of the CD). Once again, the CD must contain a barcode which must scan to match the EAN or UPC.

If your item is a DVD or VHS video. Rules that apply to music CDs are also applicable to DVD products.

Question 16. The barcode on a CD must be printed on the back in the bottom right-hand corner

A	B	C

Question 17. Pornographic products are permitted in the online sellers' programme.

A	B	C

Question 18. ISBN is short for International Standard Book Number.

A	B	C

What Criteria Do We Use to Decide if Trade Distribution is Appropriate?

Firstly, we will only consider a distribution relationship with publishers who have a UK-based storage and representation arrangement. Generally we will hold a larger stock than would normally be required of a wholesaler, but we do need to have easy access to top-up facilities within the UK.

In addition, it is imperative that the titles are represented to the trade in order to generate UK sales. Whether this is via a UK-based sales/marketing presence, or one based overseas, is not important, as long as it is effective in selling the titles to the target audience. Although we offer some promotional assistance through our weekly/monthly publications we do not offer sales and marketing as a service per se.

Minimum Turnover/Lines

The publisher should normally be able to demonstrate a realistic expectation of turnover in excess of £50k per annum at RRP and have a minimum of 5 lines. However, these targets are both negotiable where appropriate.

What Terms Will Be Required?

Final discount and credit terms will be agreed on a case-by-case basis. Stock will be held on a consignment basis and we will provide monthly statements of sales and other management information. Invoicing will be against sales achieved each month and within the credit terms agreed.

Question 19. All invoices are paid 30 days in arrears.

A	B	C

Question 20. An application from a publisher with a turnover of £49k will not be accepted.

A	B	C

Question 21. Applicants who reside in southern Ireland will not be considered for a trade account.

A	B	C

The role of the Ambulance Service

Most people believe that the Ambulance Service is simply there to respond to emergency incidents such as road traffic collisions (RTCs), seriously ill or injured patients, fires and other such incidents. While these are the core roles that the service undertakes, there are also a number of other important duties that are carried out, such as patient transport services.

The latter are is carried out by the employees of the Ambulance Service who carry disabled, elderly and vulnerable people to and from out-patient appointments, hospital admissions and also day centres and clinics. Behind the operational ambulance crew is a team of people who have different roles, all designed to provide the necessary support required that is so valued by the community.

To begin with, there are the 999 call operators who take the initial calls. Their job is to gather as much information as possible about the emergency call, the nature of the incident, its location and the level of response that is required.

These people are integral to the Ambulance Service and are crucial to patient care. For example, if a patient is critically ill they may need to talk the caller through a life-saving procedure while they wait for the ambulance crews to get there.

Question 22. The 999 call operators do not travel in the ambulance with the paramedics.

A	B	C

Question 23. Responding to road traffic collisions forms part of the core role of the Ambulance Service.

A	B	C

Question 24. 999 call operators may need to talk the caller through a lifesaving procedure while they wait for the ambulance crews to get there.

A	B	C

What is a Customer Charter?

A Customer Charter is a statement as to how a company will deliver a quality customer service. The main purpose of a Customer Charter is to inform customers of the standards of service to expect, what to do if something goes wrong and how to make a complaint. In addition to this a Customer Charter also helps employees by setting out clearly defined standards of how they should perform within the organisation in relation to customer service delivery.

Is it necessary for an organisation to have one?

Whilst not a legal requirement, a Customer Charter is an ideal way of helping organisations define with their customers, and others, what that service should be and the standard that should be expected. The charter will also help customers get the most from an organisation's services, including how to make a complaint if they are dissatisfied with any aspect of service or if they have ideas for improvement.

Other points to consider

A Customer Charter should be written in a clear and user-friendly manner.

In addition to this, a Crystal Mark endorsement by the Plain English Campaign would enhance its status. If appropriate, it should be displayed in a prominent place, so all customers can see it. The Customer Charter must be available in different formats, such as large print and audio, so that customers with particular needs can access it. If an organisation is part of an industry where a regulator has been appointed, details of how to contact the regulator should be included.

Question 25. A Customer Charter is a legal requirement within an organisation.

A	B	C

Question 26. A Customer Charter should be written using a Crystal Mark endorsement by the Plain English Campaign.

A	B	C

Question 27. The Customer Charter may be available in different formats, such as large print and audio, so that customers with particular needs can access it.

A	B	C

What is a balance sheet?

A balance sheet is a snapshot of a company's financial position at a particular point of time in contrast to an income statement, which measures income over a period of time.

A balance sheet is usually calculated for March 31, last day of the financial year. A financial year starts on April 1 and ends on March 31. For example, the period between April 1, 2011 and March 31, 2012 will complete a financial year. A balance sheet measures three kinds of variables: assets, liabilities and shareholder's equity.

Assets are things like factories and machinery that the company uses to create value for its customers. Liabilities are what the company owes to third parties (eg outstanding payments to suppliers). Equity is the money initially invested by shareholders plus the retained earnings over the years. These three variables are linked by the relationship: Assets = Liabilities + Shareholder's equity. Both assets and liabilities are further classified based on their liquidity, that is, how easily they can be converted into cash.

Current liabilities are liabilities that are due within a year and include interest payments, dividend payments and accounts payable. Long-term assets include fixed assets like land and factories as well as intangible assets like goodwill and brands. Finally, long-term liabilities are basically debt with maturity of more than a year.

Question 28 A financial year starts on March 31 and ends on April 1.

A	B	C

Question 29. It can be said that the liquidity of both assets and liabilities is how easily they can be converted into cash.

A	B	C

Question 30. A balance sheet is a legal requirement and every company must have one.

A	B	C

Answers to Verbal Reasoning

Q1. B

The sentence states that ministers hope that 'lower' inflation will boost real income growth, not higher. Therefore, the statement is false.

Q2. B

The passage states that analysts were predicting a 0.4% fall in sales of household goods, not rise. Therefore, the statement is false.

Q3. A

This statement is true based on the information provided in the passage.

Q4. B

This statement is false because the sentence states that the fire and rescue service 'may' introduce arrangements; it does not say they 'must'.

Q5. B

This statement is false because the sentence states 30th June 2008, instead of 30th June 2007 as stated in the passage.

Q6. C

We cannot say that this statement is true or false. It makes no reference in the passage that 'all' employees received a pay rise.

 how2become

Q7. A

It is true, according to the passage, that some of the characteristics of a data warehouse include integrated and non-volatile data.

Q8. B

It is possible to ascertain which employees were off sick from the information stored in a data warehouse; therefore, the statement is false.

Q9. A

It is true that corporate memory is an alternative name given to historical data.

Q10. C

The passage makes no reference to this statement. Therefore, we cannot say whether the statement is true or false from the information provided. Cannot say is the correct answer.

Q11. A

We can deduce from the passage that this statement is true.

Q12. C

In health and safety law this statement is true. However, the passage makes no reference it. Cannot say is the correct answer.

Q13. C

The passage does state that the training course is usually held over a 3-day period (18 hours). We could assume that the 18

hours are equally divided into 3 x 6 hour days. However, it is not our job to assume; we must base our answers on what is provided within the passage. Therefore, the correct answer is cannot say.

Q14. A

From the passage we know this statement to be true.

Q15. B

This statement is false because the passage states that the selection process can sometimes take longer than 12 months.

Q16. C

The passage does state that a CD will require a barcode. However, unlike the reference to the location of the barcode on books, it makes no reference to the barcode location for CDs. Therefore the answer is cannot say.

Q17. B

The passage clearly states that pornographic products are not permitted. Therefore, the correct answer is false.

Q18. C

This statement is true. However, the passage makes no reference to it. The correct answer is cannot say based on the information provided.

Q19. C

The passage makes no reference to this statement. The answer is cannot say from the information provided.

Q20. C

Although the passage makes reference to an expected turnover of £50k per annum, it also states that the targets are negotiable. Because the targets are negotiable, we cannot confirm whether the statement is true or false. As such, we must select cannot say as the correct answer.

Q21. C

The passage states that they will only consider a distribution relationship with publishers who have a UK-based storage and representation arrangement. Southern Ireland does not form part of the UK. However, the statement doesn't makes reference to applicants who 'reside' in southern Ireland. Because an applicant resides in southern Ireland we cannot say whether or not their application will be considered, simply because there is nothing to prevent a resident of southern Ireland from having a UK-based storage and representation arrangement. Therefore, the correct answer is cannot say from the information provided.

Q22. C

The passage makes no reference to this statement. The correct answer is cannot say from the information provided.

Q23. A

The passage makes it clear that responding to road traffic collisions is a core role for the Ambulance Service. The statement is true.

Q24. A

From the passage we can confirm that this statement is true.

 how2become

Q25. B

The passage clearly states that a Customer Charter is not a legal requirement. The correct answer is false.

Q26. B

The passage states that a Customer Charter should be written in a clear and user-friendly manner. It states that a Crystal Mark endorsement by the Plain English Campaign would enhance its status. Therefore, the statement is false.

Q27. B

The passage states that "The Customer Charter must be available…"

The statement above states that it 'may' be available. Therefore, it is false.

Q28. B

The statement is false because the passage states that a financial year starts on April 1 and ends on March 31. The statement is therefore false.

Q29. A

The passage clearly states that both assets and liabilities are further classified based on their liquidity, that is, how easily they can be converted into cash. The correct answer is true.

Q30. C

The passage makes no reference to this statement; therefore, cannot say is the correct answer.

Now, let's move on to the penultimate stage of the assessment centre, the GCHQ personality questionnaire.

GCHQ Personality Questionnaire

The final written assessment that you will need to take at the assessment centre, is the personality questionnaire. This is a unique exercise, which will test whether your personality is the right fit for GCHQ.

The test itself will take a number of hours to complete. The reason for this is that the test is extremely extensive. You'll be asked to complete a number of sections that require either true-false or scale-based answers to the questions. For example, a typical question from one section of the assessment might be:

I get frustrated when things aren't going my way.

True   \   False

You would be required to circle the correct answer in this instance, and then move onto the next question.

Another typical question might be:

I refuse to do things that I do not agree with.

1 / 2 / 3 / 4 / 5

In this case, the values of 1-5 would represent a particular feeling. For example, 1 would be strongly disagree, and 5 would be strongly agree, with the numbers in between making up the in between of the scale. You'd be told what the numbers represent before answering the questions.

Why do GCHQ do a personality questionnaire?

The reason that GCHQ do a personality questionnaire is because it is integral for them to establish what kind of a person you are, before you join. Generally, they will be looking for a particular type of person. Think about the competencies that we told you about earlier in the guide. When you are answering the personality questions, you should always be honest, but at the same time you need to think about how your answers will make you come across to GCHQ. For example, if you tell GCHQ that you are quick to anger, how well do you think this will sit with the assessors?

The GCHQ personality questionnaire is extremely complex, and takes hours to complete, and therefore it's impossible for us to mirror this. However, what we can do is provide you with some more sample personality questionnaire questions. Hopefully these will give you even more of an idea of what the test will be like.

Sample Personality Questionnaire Questions

1. I like to use my time as efficiently as I can.

True	False

2. I like to know what I am doing before I start something.

True	False

3. I am a reserved person.

True	False

4. People who act out on a whim annoy me.

True	False

5. I think people who act quickly are unprepared.

True	False

6. I consider myself an organised person.

True	False

7. I generally don't like taking blame for something that's gone wrong.

True	False

8. I try to avoid making mistakes by planning ahead.

True	False

9. Sometimes, I want to 'do' it instead of 'think' about it. (Reversed)

True	False

10. Always be prepared.

True	False

11. There is no such thing as over preparation.

True	False

12. I value a rational approach.

True	False

13. I don't usually blurt things out unless I've considered them carefully.

True	False

GCHQ Drugs Test

Following the completion of the assessment tests, you will be required to take a drugs test. This could consist of:

-Taking a hair sample.

-Urinating in a cup.

-Having a blood test.

In order to learn more about exactly how you will be tested, you should contact GCHQ directly.

CHAPTER 7

GCHQ Assessment

Interview

The final stage of the GCHQ Assessment Centre is the face to face interview. You will face two face-to-face interviews in the selection process for GCHQ, with the second following successful completion of the assessment centre and vetting process.

In this chapter, we will cover both of these interviews, what you should expect, the type of questions you'll be asked and provide you with in-depth sample responses to each type of interview.

The two interviews that you will face are as follows:

- The Competency Interview. This is the interview that you'll take at the assessment centre. It will last roughly 20 to 30 minutes, and will test you on your knowledge of the core competencies. You may also be asked 1 or 2 initial questions about your skillset, expertise and knowledge of the organisation.

- The Final Interview. This is the interview that you'll take following the vetting process. It will last roughly 20 minutes, and will test you on your values and motivations for wanting to join GCHQ.

Let's start with the Competency Interview.

GCHQ Competency Interview

The GCHQ Competency Interview will test you on your knowledge, understanding and application of the core competencies. You'll be asked to give specific, in-depth examples of a time when you have demonstrated a particular quality or competency. It's important to remember when answering these questions that you need to tell the interviewer what you DID do, and not what you would have done. Using this knowledge, you can prepare your answers to the competency based questions beforehand.

In order to answer these questions, you will need to have a full understanding of all the GCHQ core competencies that we mentioned earlier in this guide.

Let's recap:

• Teamwork

• Leadership and Decision Making

• Analytical Skills

• Communication

• Problem Solving

• Honesty and Integrity

How To Use The Core Competencies

When it comes to using these competencies in your responses, there are several things you need to pay careful attention to. One of the most important things you'll need in order to ensure that you pass the competency based interview, is structure. To guarantee structure, you should use the STAR interview response method.

The STAR Method:

Situation

Start off your response to the question by explaining what the 'situation' was and who was involved.

Task

Once you have detailed the situation, explain what the 'task' was, or what needed to be done.

Action

Now explain what 'action' you took, and what action others took. Also explain why you took this particular course of action.

Result

Finally, explain what the outcome or result was following your actions. Try to demonstrate in your response that the result was positive because of the action that you took.

The reason that the STAR method is so good is that it guarantees a structured response to the interview question.

Think about what happens when you go for an interview. The majority of people, naturally, are nervous. When you are nervous, you struggle to formulate a coordinated response to questions. You might talk extremely fast, miss out key information or speak about events in an incorrect order. This will detract from the interview, as you need to appear confident, relaxed and assertive.

The other reason that structure is important, is that it allows you to add extra qualities into your answers. For example, if I am answering a question that requires me to talk about a time when I worked as a member of a team, ideally I don't want to just talk about my team working abilities. At the same time, I should be aiming to show my leadership qualities, decision making and even analytical skills. Having a structured response allows us to do this, because it means that we can incorporate these competencies without creating a jumbled mess of an answer, which will confuse the interviewer. The more competencies you can demonstrate in each answer, the better, however you cannot do this without first having a good structure to your response.

Now, let's look at some typical competency based questions that you might expect to face during the interview. To help you out, we've provided you with an in-depth response to each and every single sample question.

Use the spaces we have provided you to answer the questions yourself first, and then compare your answers with ours.

Sample GCHQ Competency Questions

Q1. Can you give an example of when you have worked as part of a team, to achieve an objective or goal?

This question is centred on the core competency of teamwork. Whilst working at GCHQ, you will be part of 3 teams. Firstly, you'll be an important part of an individual unit or sector within GCHQ. Secondly, you and your unit will part of the wider GCHQ team. Thirdly, GCHQ is part of a group of individual national intelligence services, working to protect the citizens of the UK. This group includes the likes of MI5 and MI6.

What this means, in short, is that the ability to work as part of a team is an essential requirement for GCHQ applicants. It's important that you acknowledge this in your response, and that you can show a thorough understanding of the competency.

Finally, when answering a competency based question, think about what **other** competencies can be related to it. For example, teamwork relates to leadership, decision making, and good communication. The more competencies that you can work into a well-structured answer, the better. Remember to make your response as detailed as you possibly can.

Write out your answer to this question in the box provided, and then compare it with our sample response below.

Sample Response

'*When I was working in my previous position as an events manager, I was required to work in teams on a frequent basis. There were often times when I was positioned as the leader of these teams.*

On one occasion that I can remember, our task was to organise a client event. This would involve hiring out independent entertainment workers, food suppliers, health and safety specialists and other essential staff. I was one of four sub-leaders of the team, and had around 60 people under my command.

My main priority was finding the relevant healthy and safety staff. It is the responsibility of the company to ensure that they have met recognised safety standards, and to maintain the wellbeing of all attendees at their event. In the event of an injury, a failure to implement health and safety procedures could seriously damage the business. I made contact with the paramedical department of the local hospital, and requested for them to free up several members of staff and at least four vehicles, for the day of the event. I then liaised with all 3 of the other team leaders, to ensure that I had all of the details of exactly what they were planning. Between us, we worked out exactly which health and safety procedures would need to be put in place to accommodate the activities being arranged. Following this meeting, I instructed the team under my control to make contact with the local fire service, and the local police service, and request for staff members from each sector to be available on the day of the event. We successfully negotiated a time and fee.

The event was a tremendous success. At the end of the day,

I was congratulated by my boss on my efforts in securing the participation of these crucial safety management services. The client was extremely happy and went on to book 3 more future events, using our company.'

Q2. Can you give me an example of a time when you have demonstrated your communicational abilities?

This is another question you should absolutely expect to hear during the competency based interview. As we have mentioned, communication is extremely important when working at GCHQ. This applies to both spoken and written communication. The latter especially will play a huge role in how successful you are, as the quality of your written communication will impact heavily on the standard of your written reports.

Write out your answer to this question in the box provided, and then compare it with our sample response below.

Sample Response

'During the training for my previous role as an administrator, I was required to perform a group presentation. This presentation formed an essential part of the probationary period, and therefore it was crucial that myself and my team received a high mark.

I had been placed into a presentation group with 3 foreign staff members, who still had yet to gain a full grasp of the English language. When you are presenting, you are awarded marks for communication. Therefore a failure to speak in clear, English sentences could have resulted in us being penalised. I realised that, in order for us to succeed, I would have to take leadership of the group. I arranged an initial meeting in order to establish what roles everyone would have in the presentation, and to establish what their strengths and weaknesses were. Following this, I wrote up a detailed action plan and report that outlined all of the things that everyone would be doing, and the way that they should go about doing this. It was my belief that this would give us a clear strategy.

I strongly felt that it was important for every single member of the group to demonstrate that they could communicate effectively, and speak in the presentation. Therefore I wrote out some very basic material for them to read, so everyone would gain a communication mark. When it came to the presentation, I took on the majority of the speaking, but made sure that everyone else had a turn.

Without my input, I feel that the members of the team would have struggled to communicate or even organise a meeting. I was responsible for organising which part of the presentation each member would be responsible for, as well as creating

PowerPoint slides and written content. We ultimately received a distinction for the presentation, and every single member of the group successfully completed their probationary training.'

Q3. Analytical skills are extremely important in this line of work. Can you give us an example of a time when you have analysed specific data, in order to make changes/ improvements?

During your role as a GCHQ Intelligence Analyst, you will need to use your analytical skills on a daily basis. You will need to analyse data, and weigh up the pros and cons behind key decisions, before constructing proposal documents and reports.

A good example of this can be seen in the case analysis questions that you practiced earlier in this test. Think about the way that the questions required you to use logic and analysis to reach sensible and informed decisions. This practice of narrowing down options, and carefully weighing up which decision makes the most sense, is similar to the type of analysis you'll be required to perform at GCHQ (although it goes without saying that the issues GCHQ deal with are a great deal more complex).

Write out your answer to this question in the box provided, and then compare it with our sample response below.

Sample Response

'Whilst working as an administrator at my previous company, I was part of the team responsible for organising client events. The company is one of the top providers of business software in the UK, and therefore client events are extremely important for pushing products and increasing revenue. We frequently host events that feature motivational and expert speakers, which are attended by both new and pre-existing clients.

From 2013 till 2014, we noticed that there was a drop in the attendance of these events. Coincidentally, we suffered from a loss of revenue with pre-existing clients not paying for updates/new software, and a lack of new customers. I was tasked with fixing this. When it came to planning the 2015 event, I knew that it was extremely important to boost attendances again. With the help of my team, we interviewed the sales representatives at the company.

They felt that there a lack of direct advertising and marketing for the events, and that if we wanted to boost attendance, we needed to use social media to make people more aware that the events were taking place. I personally wrote up a questionnaire, which was dispatched to past attendees of our events, requesting feedback on how the events could be improved. Based on this feedback, I drew up an entirely new network and marketing plan for the events. This included improving the social media coverage of the event, and hiring social media experts to increase its exposure.

The end result of this was that, for our 2015 events, we broke our own record for attendances. Our client base responded extremely well to the improved social media coverage, and this resulted in a huge increase in revenue for the year.

Feedback reports said that the client base was very happy with the improved networking strategy, and that they would be highly likely to recommend such events to their friends and family'.

Q4. GCHQ Intelligence Analysts often have to make difficult decisions. Tell us about a time in your personal or professional life, when you have had to make a difficult decision. How did you arrive at your decision?

As the question states, when working as an Intelligence Analyst, there will often be times when you are required to make difficult decisions. This doesn't just relate to writing reports or proposals either, sometimes the difficult decisions that you make will just come down to the way in which you analyse a particular piece of data.

Working at GCHQ is an extremely exciting and varied career, but it is also incredibly difficult. The level of analysis that you'll have to perform in your real day-to-day life is far beyond anything that we can accurately portray in this book, and that is why it's important that you already have experience of decision making and analysis. GCHQ need to know that they are hiring someone who won't have difficultly taking initiative and responsibility, who won't shy away from challenges and difficult/complex puzzles.

Write out your answer to this question in the box provided, and then compare it with our sample response below.

Sample Response

'During my time as an administrator, I was often required to make difficult decisions. One such occasion that I can remember was when a member of my team turned up to work in an inebriated state.

The individual in question had undergone severe personal trauma. While he had been offered time off to deal with this, he had refused. Some of the other members of the management team felt that the best course of action was to send him home and release him from the company. They were uncomfortable with his behaviour and believed that, because he refused to take time off, attending the office in this state was extremely unprofessional. I was ultimately tasked with making the decision on what to do with the employee.

My first decision was what to do with the employee on an immediate basis. While I would certainly be sending him home, I decided that my options were a) to call the police, b) to assign someone from the office to take him home, or c) to use a contact number for someone to collect him and take him home. I decided upon option C. While there were a number of willing volunteers, I did not want to further damage the day's work. A relative of the employee arrived swiftly and took him home in her car.

My second decision was whether the employee should be sacked. I weighed up all of the options before making this decision. If we fired him, we would be showing a lack of sensitivity and understanding as a company. If we did not fire him, we might be setting a bad example. I ultimately decided that I was prepared to give him one final chance, since this was the first time it had happened.

The individual in question was a very capable employee and losing him would only damage the business. I called the employee the next morning, and spoke to him about the situation. I informed him in a sensitive manner that if he wished to keep his job, then he a) needed to take some time off to deal with his issue, and b) needed to use this time to seek therapy or guidance. I reassured him that the company would support him through this difficult period in his life.

The end result of this situation was that the employee took a two week break, and came back feeling better. He is still at the company, and has now risen to a management position. I believe that by making measured decisions, I ultimately aided the company long term'.

Q5. Can you give me an example of a time when you have demonstrated your integrity and professionalism?

As we have mentioned, professionalism and integrity are extremely important for any aspiring GCHQ candidate. The nature of the organisation means that GCHQ must be able to trust you before they can hire you, or allow you access to top secret security information.

Furthermore, it's vital that you can behave in a manner that matches the GCHQ code of discretion. Failure to comply with this won't just endanger your job security, but will also endanger the lives of those around you, and of the British public.

Write out your answer to this question in the box provided, and then compare it with our sample response below.

Sample Response

'Whilst working for a voluntary agency, I was assigned to assist an elderly, ethnic homeless woman in selecting some new clothes. Whilst I was helping her, a gang of teenagers entered the shop. They started to make racist comments towards the woman. I was disgusted by this, and extremely concerned for the individual to whom they were addressing their remarks. I was determined to put a stop to it, and protect the woman.

The first thing that I did was to stand between the woman and the racist individuals, to shield her from any further comments or abuse. I told the individuals that their comments were not acceptable, and that they were in conflict with the law.

I then called over the shop manager for assistance. He immediately rang the police, and asked the teenagers to leave the store. He informed me that the shop CCTV cameras would have recorded the offending individuals, and therefore the police would be able to handle the issue from there. After the individuals had left, the manager took me and the elderly lady in the back of the shop, sat us down and made the woman a coffee. I comforted her and informed her that I would be happy to act as a witness for what I had just seen.

The end result of this was that the individuals in question were prosecuted in court, and the woman did not suffer any further abuse. I believe that my actions were imperative in comforting, supporting and making her feel as if she was protected from their racist behaviour, and that this displayed my integrity as a professional, and a human being.'

Further Vetting & Final Interview

If you are successful in your assessment centre interview, you will then face a significant waiting period. During this period, GCHQ will conduct an extensive vetting process on you and your background. In some cases, this could last up to 6 months, so you will need to remain patient. You can expect the organisation to conduct a thorough check on everything that you've included in your CV, including grades, employment dates and references.

Following the vetting process, if you are successful, you will be invited back for one final interview. This interview will be different to the previous one, in that it will not be competency based. Instead, this interview will focus on your values, your motivations for joining GCHQ, and your knowledge of the organisation.

If you have reached this stage, then you can be confident that GCHQ are seriously considering employing you. However, don't be too relaxed, as the challenge isn't over yet. The final step that you need to take is in convincing them that you are the right person to join their organisation. That is the purpose of this interview.

Now, let's take a look at some sample questions.

Q1. Tell Me About Yourself

This is a typical opening question, which gives you a great opportunity to talk about yourself, your interests and your background. The best way to answer this is to structure your response in a clear and concise manner. Start with your early qualifications, then any key work experience, and finally list your recent accomplishments. By structuring your response, you will guarantee that the interviewer gets a clear idea of who you are and how your personal qualities will help you to perform the role.

Using the above information, write your answer to this question in the box provided, and then compare it with the sample response below.

Sample Response

'I'm a logical and sensible person, who has always been interested in solving difficult puzzles. I have a highly analytical brain, and have utilised this ability on many occasions in my life. I have high grades in GCSE English, Maths, Psychology, IT, German and French, and followed both of the latter, English and Psychology up to A Level. As a result, I'm multilingual, a fantastic written and verbal communicator, and someone who has an excellent understanding of human behaviour.

I spent a significant period after my school years working in a cyber security company. I moved up from internship to a mid-level position within the organisation, which taught me a huge amount about data analytics and computer coding. I followed this up with a Cyber Security Management degree at University, where I achieved a First at undergraduate level, and subsequently moved on to complete a further Masters in the subject. I absolutely loved my degree and am now looking for the opportunity to use the skills that I picked up from this, in the workplace.

Following my postgraduate studies, I worked as an administrative assistant for a leading business consulting company in Canary Wharf. Whilst in this position, I was part of and led, multiple teams. On several occasions, I led my own team to monthly, company based awards. After working in this position for several years, and reaching a high rank within the company, I have decided that it is time to move on and test my skills elsewhere.

It has always been my ambition to protect people from threats such as cybercrime and terrorism, and I believe this position would provide me with the opportunity to do that'.

Q2. What do you know about our organisation?

This is another commonly asked question. Here, the interviewer wants to know that you have done your research on GCHQ prior to the interview. You don't have to know the organisation inside out, but you should always make sure that you have a good idea of the work that they do. If you can't answer this question in an accurate manner, then it will come across as if you have not done any research, or that you are uninterested or unenthusiastic. Make specific reference to real statistics, such as the fact that GCHQ have prevented up to 7 attacks in the last year alone.

Show that you agree with the ethos and values of the organisation, and that you have great respect and admiration for the way in which they protect the safety of the British and global populous. If you can provide evidence that you have conducted detailed research into exactly how GCHQ contribute to solving problems, then you will really impress the interviewers. Finally, remember to emphasise your ability to adhere to secrecy and discretion.

Using the above information, write your answer to this question in the box provided, and then compare it with the sample response below.

Sample Response

'I know that you are an absolutely integral element of British National Security, and that is one of the things that most attracts me about working for this organisation.

I have conducted detailed research into the work that GCHQ does, and was hugely impressed. In particular, the fact that GCHQ have prevented 7 attacks in the last year speaks volumes to me about the value of the organisation. It is essential that British citizens feel safe not only on their own soil, but in other countries too, and that is why I am grateful on a personal level for the work that GCHQ do. Now, I want to give something back. Without the efforts of GCHQ intelligence, thousands of lives could have been lost. It is my aim to become an integral cog in this security blanket, by forging a successful career with GCHQ.'

Q3. What are your biggest strengths?

This is a great question for you, as it allows you to highlight your best qualities. Make sure that your answer is relevant to the role. As we have mentioned, you should tailor your response to the core competencies. A good answer to this question tells the interviewer that your biggest strengths are: your analytical reasoning, your communication, your ability to make good decisions and your ability to work as part of a team.

While it's all well and good if you are a caring and loving person, this isn't one of the requirements for the role and therefore it doesn't need to be mentioned. You could also tell the interviewer that you have a fantastic ability to deal with complex and difficult situations.

Using the above information, write your answer to this question in the box provided, and then compare it with the sample response below.

Sample Response

'*I believe that I have several key strengths, all of which make me a good fit for your organisation: Firstly, I have an extremely analytical mind and I am capable of making fast, logical and well considered decisions. I have a wealth of experience in making decisions where there were a number of variables to assess under tight time constraints; and the overwhelming majority of these decisions resulted in a positive outcome.*

Secondly, I am an excellent team worker. As I progressed through the ranks of my previous company, I was assigned leadership of several teams, and this enabled me to put my great decision making skills into practice. This quality has also really helped me to stay organised in the past, especially when it came to organising events, filing company reports and making sure that I worked ahead of schedule.

Finally, I have fantastic communicational abilities. This proved essential in my previous role as an administrator, as I spent the majority of my days in constant communication with customers, and with the other members of my team. In particular my written report and proposal writing is extremely strong, and I have never had any issues with putting my message across in a clear and decisive manner.

I believe that all of my strengths are well suited for the role of an Intelligence Analyst, and that this is a position which would allow me to perform to the absolute best of my ability'.

Q4. What is your biggest weakness?

When answering this question, you need to show a level of personal awareness, without making yourself seem too flawed as a candidate. The worst thing you can say here is, 'I have no weaknesses'. This will show a lack of personal understanding to the interviewer, and could be particularly damning if you are applying for a role such as Intelligence Analyst, where you will work as part of a team.

Try to select one weakness, which you believe working for the organisation will improve. Alternatively, select a weakness which you have already taken steps to improve, and show how you have done it. Make sure that the weakness you select is something that will not severely damage your ability to perform the role; the key is to show that you are someone who recognises their own limitations and responds accordingly.

Using the above information, write your answer to this question in the box provided, and then compare it with the sample response below.

Sample Response

'My biggest weakness is that I have been known, at times, to put too much responsibility on myself. I'm someone who always wants to see a job done properly, and therefore I have a tendency to avoid delegating tasks to anyone else. This was particularly an issue when I started in my previous role. On one occasion I was placed in a team with three others. After two weeks, it became apparent that the other members of the team were discontented. This was because I had taken too much work, and not left them enough to do. We had a group meeting to resolve the issue and I quickly realised my mistake. I'm working very hard to fix this, as I know that working in a team is a vital requirement for an Intelligence Analyst'.

Q5. Do you have any questions for me?

This is an essential part of any interview, and is an area in which many candidates fall down. They don't come into the interview prepared to ask questions, and are caught off guard by this. Many candidates simply respond with 'no' or 'I think you've told me everything I need to hear.' This is a critical mistake! By not asking questions, you are showing a lack of enthusiasm and interest to the employer. You are showing them that you don't really care enough to find out more about them.

GCHQ want you to ask questions. They want to know that you care, and that their organisation has captured your interest. Before your interview, formulate a list of at least 7 questions that you want to ask the organisation at the end of the interview. That way, even if 1 or 2 or your questions are covered during the interview, you will still have some left in reserve. Make sure to listen keenly to their answers, and even be prepared to ask short questions based on their responses.

Here are a list of general interview questions, which you can ask any employer:

• What on-the-job training will I receive?

• If I was successful in my application, what would you expect from me? How fast would you expect me to develop my skills?

• Is there an opportunity for progression in the position I am applying for?

• I see that you won a recent award for...? Can you tell me more about this?

• Do you have any reservations about my ability to do the job?

• What are the future goals of the company? How do you see my role fitting within those goals?

CHAPTER 8

A Few Final Words

You have now reached the end of this guide and no doubt will be ready to start preparing for the GCHQ intelligence analyst selection process. Before you start your preparation, consider the following common attributes that the majority of successful candidates possess:

1. They believe in themselves.

The first factor is self-belief. Regardless of what anyone tells you, you can become an intelligence analyst. Just like any job, you have to be prepared to work hard in order to be successful. Do everything you can to pass the selection process and fill your mind with positive thoughts.

2. They prepare fully.

The second factor is preparation. The biggest achievers in life prepare fully for every eventuality, and that is what you must do when you apply to become a GCHQ Intelligence Analyst. Work hard, and concentrate on improving your weakest areas.

3. They persevere.

Everybody comes across obstacles or setbacks in their life, but it is what you do about those setbacks that is important. If you fail at something, then ask yourself *'why'* you have failed. This will allow you to improve for next time. If you keep improving, success will follow.

4. They are self-motivated.

How much do you want this job? Do you want it, or do you *really* want it? When you apply to join GCHQ, you should want it more than anything in the world. During the weeks

and months leading up to the GCHQ selection process, keep yourself motivated, eat healthy and maintain your fitness levels.

By working hard and staying focused, you can achieve anything that you set your mind to!

Get more books, manuals, online

tests and training courses at:

www.how2become.com